New, Improved?

New, Improved?

Exposing the misuse of popular psychology

ARIC SIGMAN

SIMON & SCHUSTER

LONDON · SYDNEY · NEW YORK · TOKYO · SINGAPORE · TORONTO

First published in Great Britain by Simon & Schuster Ltd, 1995
A Paramount Communications Company

Simon & Schuster Ltd
West Garden Place
Kendal Street
London W2 2AQ

Simon & Schuster of Australia Pty Ltd
Sydney
A CIP catalogue record for this book is available
from the British Library.

ISBN 0–671-71380-9

Typeset in Meridien by Hewer Text Composition Services, Edinburgh
Printed and bound in Great Britain by
Butler & Tanner Ltd, Frome and London

I WISH I WERE IN LOVE AGAIN

Acknowledgements

I would like to thank my assistant Sarah Wragg not only for preparing the manuscript but for contributing many a useful turn of phrase; in particular, the term used to describe the dress code for today's chic radical – 'Gothic Playschool'. Despite her aversion to being described as 'sensible', it was, much to her chagrin, precisely this quality which I found immensely helpful.

I am most grateful to my editor Jo Frank for commissioning this book and allowing me to express myself with a minimum of interference. Moreover, despite her 'liberal' proclivities (and her Islington address), she has remained remarkably impartial and good-humoured over the political tone of much of this book.

Contents

1: Great Expectations

Psychology has been catapulted into everyday language in a relatively short space of time. A glance backwards to the post-McCarthy era psychology that dominated the public's consciousness conjures up images of the psychologist as a cold, B-Movie type of rational scientist in white coat and glasses, engaging in subliminal advertising experiments, hypnosis, electric shock therapy and 'brainwashing' – all the virtues which inspired me to go into psychology as a boy.

My adolescent years were, however, spent in the New England setting which John Updike was making a rather nice living writing about. Our neighbourhood was littered with academics, interspersed with a few executives and even the odd vicar sprinkled here and there. It was the summer of 1970, a year after Woodstock and the new ideas had had sufficient time to sink in. Life in our road was not uninteresting, 'musical beds' being a favoured indulgence. The then wife of the man living in the imposing house on the other side of the road ran off with the husband of her next-door-neighbour, whose deceived wife in turn found consolation in bed with the mature bisexual female college student lodging in our attic, who was herself very sexually generous toward my needs, not to mention those of several of my brothers. Predictably, the vicar who lived three houses down abandoned his wife, five children and flock and began worshipping a 22-year-old pair of heavenly bosoms.

'Musical potted plants' was another favoured hobby. My mother noticed that one of my younger brothers had apparently developed a keen interest in horticulture, a hobby which involved humidifiers and ultra-violet lights in the basement. In

1

an attempt to be an 'involved parent' and to further encourage my brother's interest in all things environmental, she dutifully got a book about exotic plants. After setting about trying to match the pictures in the book with the resplendent foliage before her, she triumphantly identified my brother's exotic leafy specimen. Its Latin name was most impressive: *cannabis sativa* 'a plant of the mulberry family'. However, as her eyes fixed upon the various translations: '*marijuana, hashish, ganja*' she quickly realised she would have to redefine what being an 'involved parent' meant to her. The plants were thrown out summarily. However, the college student living next door, believing that 'plants have feelings too', felt sorry for them and took them in. Unfortunately the owner of the house also had a book about exotic plants, but he too respected their feelings and those of young, budding horticulturalists, and quietly offered them to my brother whereby, through a circuitous route, they ended up back in their ultra-violet home.

The man who kindly returned the *cannabis sativa* was a medical academic. He was not however your average New England medical professor. George was warm, caring, communicative and openly loving toward his wife and children: in essence, a 'new man' twenty years before the term even originated. His wife, Judith, was the local feminist and was rather partial to group therapy and growth (though I'm sure that in a previous era she would have been an active member of the WI). Judith was on rather good terms with her group therapist, Ben, who I was to discover availed himself for 'home visits'. I remember an occasion when he dropped in to see her, knocked on the open door but found there was no answer. As he stuck his head in, he could hear running water and thought she was probably doing a bit of washing up. It never occurred to the silly man that feminists didn't do the washing up, rather, they took communal, platonic showers with other feminists. He proceeded down the hallway

2

to discover, to his delight, both Judith and her female lodger scrubbing each other's back. Feeling that this was the perfect moment to hold an impromptu encounter group, he took off his clothes and joined them to better enable him to 'relate' to them. To me, the strangest part of this group therapy was that it did indeed remain communal and platonic, such was the pretentious ethos of that era.

It was at this point that I began to suspect that psychology was not about electric shock therapy and subliminal advertising.

Believing that one's husband could never possess too much of a good thing and that there is always room for renewal and improvement, one day Judith suggested George go off for an upcoming weekend of 'personal growth through developing greater sensitivity'. Being the caring, sharing, supportive chap he was, he was of course happy to accommodate her wishes.

Although my father was also a medical academic, he had little in common with George. While he was a terribly honest, noble and principled man, a verbose man he was certainly not. He would be voted 'Least Likely Man To Engage In Recreational Weeping'. He oozed machismo, being both authoritative *and* authoritarian; he was Post-McCarthy Man. The world of encounter groups and 'growth' was a complete anathema to him, if not an outright nightmare. Therapists were 'chiropractors of the mind'. He was soon to have all of his suspicions confirmed, for the 'new' psychology was about to be played out in our very own driveway.

As our family were preparing to go out one evening, George was just returning from his weekend of self-discovery at the sensitivity farm. He seemed unusually gleeful, brandishing that constant LSD type of smile that one apparently adopts at the point of self-actualisation, giggling, buoyant and 'high on life'. It was obvious that he wanted to *share* his happiness with someone and who better than his good neighbour . . . my father. As George drew closer to my father, who was at this point becoming most suspicious, he announced joyfully: 'Life is wonderful, we're all part of one universe – you, me, the earth, the moon and the stars . . . what I'm trying to tell you is, I feel close to you . . . Edmund, I love you!' Catching my father off-guard, he embraced and kissed him. For a moment my father stood rigid and unresponsive then, recoiling in horror, blurted out: 'For God's sake, pull yourself together George!!! . . . What on earth's gotten into you?' Judith laughed with that 'my-husband's-more-sensitive-than-yours' look on her face. Psychology had finally arrived in our driveway; it had even become part of keeping-up-with-the-Joneses.

The psychology of the next decade held further surprises for me. The 1970s saw a blurring of the distinction between the worlds of psychology, sociology, social work, education and civil rights with terms such as 'empowerment', 'rights', 'self-expression', 'abuse', 'self-esteem', 'stereotyping', 'taking responsibility', 'victimology' as well as various 'isms', all being passed back and forth and taking on political connotations to finally evolve into moral imperatives with local government backing. Psychology was invoked to help change society. I became aware of this when taking part in a typical 1970s social experiment designed to help reform 'problem' young people by dissuading them from shooting up heroin, selling their bodies, mugging old ladies or stabbing members of the general public and to replace these socially undesirable activities with healthy pastimes such as ping-pong, playing cards and generally working for a living. This was a rather tall order as the 'young people' in question were actually aged between 18 and 26, most were Glaswegian ex-offenders with tattoos which were more like murals covering large areas of their anatomy. The 'project' took place in a club which was open in the evenings and a small subsidised bar was provided in order to draw in the clientele in need. Every hour was 'Happy Hour'. The staff comprised two social workers in the making, two 'youth leaders', one or two counsellors and two would-be psychologists. Donkey jackets and wire-rimmed spectacles were considered a good career move; even first names were thought somewhat formal and were often replaced by 'brutha' as a universal term of address. The Club Director was a northern socialist who spent much of his time closeted in his quarters on the third floor which was also frequented by the local Catholic priest who often spent the night. It would seem unlikely that they were holding their own private confession as the Club Director was a Protestant.

The second-in-command, Phil, one of the up-and-coming social workers, best exemplified the rich cross-fertilisation of our respective fields. Sporting the aforementioned garb and to ensure that it was clear to all concerned that he was a committed 'brutha', he sported a little socialist beard – his face looked like a winter of discontent. Phil believed that the best way of cultivating the desired new and improved attitudes was to run the club by a form of democratic consensus; a somewhat urban version of *Animal Farm*. It was therefore of paramount importance to avoid being 'authoritarian', rather, one should be 'sensitive to the needs of the individual'. Phil spent his spare evenings reading *The Use of Empathy in the Emotional Transformation of Orwellian Reprobates*. I, on the other hand, sent off for details of evening classes in unarmed combat.

'Pet', the petulant prostitute from Paisley, attired in leather trousers, a sleeveless, studded leather waistcoat which revealed her muraled biceps, and sporting a neo-mohican hairstyle, did not appear to have much difficulty in 'expressing her emotions'. On one occasion, a fellow young person who had a difference of opinion with her met with a broken bottle planted in the side of his neck. Phil, however, *The Use of Empathy in the Emotional Transformation of Orwellian Reprobates* in hand, felt that he could somehow 'connect' with her, and was in fact proved right by Pet who showed her appreciation of his efforts by connecting her fist with his face thus breaking his wire-rimmed spectacles. Phil no doubt viewed this as a form of 'client feedback'. Fortunately Pet had different plans for me. Noticing that I had been furiously engaged in weight training, she challenged me to an arm wrestling match which, after a struggle, I won. To convey both her amazement and admiration at her defeat, I was rewarded with the offer of 'a trick on the house, Jimmy'. Putting my spectacles carefully back into their case, I declined her kind offer.

As in *Animal Farm*, the project ended in anarchy with the 'animals' taking over the club and barricading themselves in. They gave themselves up though when the beer ran out, and the club closed for an extended period of 're-education'.

The most graphic example of the lucrative misappropriation of psychological concepts occurred during the 1980s and is currently to be found within the 'profession' which refers to itself as 'management consultancy'. Those unfamiliar with this term may be interested to know that *anyone*, including Frank Bruno, would be entitled to call themselves a 'management consultant'. Organisations, both public and private, spend hundreds of millions of pounds each year to establish the latest psychological thought on 'stress management', 'assertiveness training', 'neurolinguistic programming' or 'managing change'. Such 'management development' can, for example, be found in the form of courses entitled 'The Sensitive Manager', during which the boorish, middle-aged corporate weasel (or weaselette) spends a week of self-discovery at a sensitivity farm, to return as a caring, sharing, supportive human being. A more rugged approach is known as the Outward Bound type of course, over which enlightenment is achieved through abseiling, paragliding and getting lost on mountainsides with one's colleagues. The recession of the early 1990s produced the most divine example of 'positive-thinking-meets-board-of-directors', when management consultants, trying to prevent a lowering of morale as a result of mass redundancies, suggested that the process of 'down-sizing' be referred to in future as 'right-sizing'.

The new psychology is now featured within the National Health Service. General practitioners have more recently been encouraged to respond to the emotional aspects of their patients' discomfiture − 'to treat patients as whole individuals' − and as such have been indoctrinated by the current ideas within counselling. Many GPs now attend courses on counselling, which they believe, like medical school, teach 'techniques' which are scientifically testable and based in fact. An acquaintance of mine who wanted to better prepare himself to counsel couples who may be experiencing marital difficulties is a good case in point. Aware of the spiralling rate of divorce, he attended the prescribed relationship counselling course where he learned the importance of promoting 'openness' and 'honesty' within relationships.

One day in his surgery he was confronted by a couple who had been his patients for some time; on this occasion, however, they looked decidedly grim. It transpired that the wife had been caught having an affair with a family friend 'because her husband had been inattentive, away on business a lot'. The GP observed that there had been a serious 'breakdown in trust' and that if the relationship were to survive, great attempts would have to be made by both parties to 'rebuild that trust'. It was therefore imperative − in order to wash away the remnants of deceit − that they should, from this point onward, be 'completely and utterly honest with one another'. However, a week later, they arrived back in his surgery in a worse state. Honesty appeared to have rather strange side effects; these became apparent as they recounted the week's events; these included the following trust-rebuilding conversation:

Husband: You heard what the doctor said, we want to be honest with one another . . . So, was the other guy's bigger than mine?

Wife: Well . . . umm, actually I'm afraid it was.

Husband: Bastard! How much bigger?

Wife: About two and a half inches longer and the circumference was about . . .

Husband: That's enough! I don't want to hear any more! Where did you do it with him, was it in our marital bed, the way we do it?

Wife: Of course not, darling, I thought it best to avoid the missionary position altogether . . . so we did it over the back of the chair in your study and he drilled me from behind over the sofa . . .

Husband: Stop! Stop! I don't want to go any further . . . What else did you do with him? I want to know everything – doctor's orders!

Wife: Well, umm . . . I sucked him.

Husband: You did what? Did you let him come in your mouth?

Wife: Yes, but I only swallowed half of it and I made him squirt
the rest of it on my breasts and then rub it in – *Marie Claire* said
it was good for my skin . . .

It appeared that, as their new, improved, more honest relationship developed, the husband was becoming evermore obsessed
with his wife's specific adulterous 'crimes', wanting to know
every detail in order to rationalise the infidelity and to compare
himself to the other man. Their GP was in a quandary, for as
the husband had become more distrustful, it wasn't possible to
call the woman back in for a private consultation in order to
prescribe some alternative medicine to help salvage her marriage
– to tell her to *lie* from there on in.

More recently, the hijacking of psychology by mainstream
media has come to grotesque fruition in the genre of confession
television, featuring rhinestone-clad victims who live out the
media-approved current line in emotional disabilities, thereby
raising their self-esteem over the 15 minutes of fame to which
they feel entitled. The world of TV 'dysfunctionals' has become
so competitive that talent agencies have been set up to classify
and cross-reference every disorder on computer to ensure that
television producers can be provided with the latest combina-
tions available on the circuit.

Psychology now has international political implications. There
has been a call within the British Psychological Society by Dr
Bill Puplampu of the University of Westminster for the greater
use of psychology in developing countries. 'We must explicate a
psychology with a clear, politically defined role . . . [with a] brief
to confront and comment on the process of government. . . .
This must go hand in hand with involvement in local, regional,
national councils and parliaments and direct confrontation.'
Where this is not possible, Dr Puplampu suggests 'we may

pursue a psychology where the emphasis is on using our theories and methods to influence community and individual development processes – career guidance, self-help projects etc.' The academic literature which surrounds this issue comes in the form of titles such as *Asserting Psychology in Africa* or alternatively *Asserting Psychology in Malawi*.

It has come to the point where it is increasingly unnecessary to distinguish between popular or public psychology and the more realistic variety based in responsible research. The only psychology that reaches the public domain, including the well educated, *is* a public version. Academic psychology is, on the whole, terribly dull and even when it isn't, the way it is written up ensures that it will end up that way; few would want to be exposed to the genuine article for this reason. Therefore, when one speaks of psychology, it is really a form of public psychology.

The media is one of the main routes by which public psychology and the values derived from it reach the public consciousness. Unfortunately, psychologists are notoriously inept at countering these influences. Dr Margaret Mitchell, the Honorary Press Officer of the British Psychological Society, laments: 'Texts in newspapers often include the words "psychologically" or "psychologists would say" and attribute opinions with which psychologists might agree, but would very often not . . . we really must set ourselves against this sort of quasi-psychological rubbish.'

Between the state, the Church and the individual, lie what Edmund Burke referred to as 'the little platoons of society' – those influences and institutions which enable people to breathe in values. Unfortunately many of these values, often couched in and reinforced through the use of psychological terms, reflect what can only be referred to as an 'editorial line' regarding the human condition: the psychology that makes its way into social and corporate structures reflects the way certain interested parties would like things to be. As a result, erroneous ideas concerning more 'beneficial' ways to feel, behave and love have become deeply engrained in our culture, from the Arts and the entertainment world to the major institutions involved in everything from marriage guidance to safer sex, civil rights to government policy.

The backdrop to this is a society exposed endlessly to a torrent of 'data', 'information', 'research', and 'statistics' from the myriad interested sources; their scepticism often being indistinguishable from their gullibility. Everything, from what we eat to how we vote and to our sexual behaviour, is analysed by people with a vested interest in reaching preselected conclusions. As Cynthia Crossen, author of *Tainted Truth: The Corruption of Fact in the Information Age*, states, 'In the information business, truth belongs to those who commission it.' Psychology is no exception. Everyone has, in varying degrees, unconsciously absorbed ideas about happiness and fulfilment, many of which only make us feel inadequate. The public have taken these ideas on board without challenging, or even thinking about them.

In the promotion of any form of knowledge it is often the least academic who are best at communicating, persuading or selling. *The World Tonight*, BBC Radio 4's sombre nightly news at ten programme – one of the little platoons – is well aware of this. On 6 January 1994, the Government was reeling from the deafening sound of yet another pair of ministerial trousers dropping. Tim Yeo, Environment Minister, was forced to resign because of a sex scandal, and *The World Tonight* had a main feature on adultery, with informed, expert opinion provided by the editor of *Cosmopolitan*. The producers of prime-time soap operas when addressing current issues routinely seek the advice of other little platoons to gen up on the latest editorial line to convey. User-friendly scenarios with rather unsubtle social messages concerning lesbianism, child sexual

11

abuse, drug addiction, racism, HIV/AIDS and safer sex help 'raise the public's awareness' by assisting it in adopting the 'appropriate' attitudes toward these and many more subtle issues. Art imitating delusion.

Inherent in the editorial line of the prevailing psychology are a variety of leanings; consistent themes which though attractive, reassuring and politically desirable, are ultimately at odds with reality. Most of the psychological concepts, as well as the capacity for exploiting them, have naturally come from the United States. American 'things', whether they be tangible goods, or ideas concerning the human condition, are immensely appealing. America is the master of contagious veneer, design and marketing. Which other nation could persuade the world not only to wear baseball caps, but to wear them the wrong way around? American psychology emphasises man's potential for self-direction and freedom of choice which, like the 'classless society', have a certain democratic ring to them, being far more appealing than European accounts of the human condition. The suggestion of a 'new way' to conduct one's life, enabling one to 'manage' the way one thinks, reacts and feels, is seductive in providing a fresh start without the emotional baggage and limited horizons provided by a long-standing class system or a difficult childhood. However, the introduction of such notions into Britain has failed to take into account profound cultural differences between Britain and America. This is a significant problem for the British who can't even manage to 'Have A Nice Day'; even the Americans have, at least on a subconscious level, started to ask questions about the availability of The American Dream.

Psychology has also suffered from a female bias. While it is claimed that 'it's a man's world', this has certainly not been the case within contemporary psychology. A report by the British Psychological Society entitled *Psychology and its students* stated: 'Within psychology, two main trends of the last couple of decades continue. One is that psychology is becoming ever more female . . . In most advanced countries they outnumber men.' Female student members outnumber males by four to one. Almost three quarters of the members of The British Association For Counselling are women and RELATE Marriage Guidance also reports a definite shortage of male counsellors. It is therefore not surprising that a male perspective on areas such as relationships and sex is sadly lacking. Moreover, those men who, as RELATE phrased it, 'put themselves forward to become counsellors', or write and broadcast about such matters, are rather unlikely to have a rich history of wifebeating. Few men ever read about emotional issues, the demographic profile of magazine and book readers makes this abundantly clear. The professional world of dealing with emotions, including the consumers of its products and services, has been a female domain; a point so obvious that it has been completely overlooked as a significant issue. Like male designers in the fashion world, those men within the 'feeling' industry are hardly representative of men in general. Male therapists, counsellors and psychologists who discuss emotional issues publicly, tend to be more happy to tow the accepted line. Having bought into the system, such men can expect to be approved of and admired by 'wimmin'. This state of affairs has unfortunately provided society with a distorted frame of reference in which to consider feelings and behaviour, thus causing a great deal of confusion, unfulfilled expectations and pain. There can be no 'genderless' psychology: there are two realities; one for men and one for women.

It has been most fashionable as of late to deride 'therapy'. However, as only a small minority of people are actually involved in therapy, recent critics have missed the point entirely. Their preoccupation with the question of whether therapy is effective and ethical has subsumed a much more relevant issue, extending far beyond the therapist's chamber, insidiously affecting a broader range of people. While at one time, therapy was an approach for dealing with serious psychological problems, 'mental illness', the only people finding themselves at the wrong end of a therapist's couch tended to be in rather a bad way. Therapeutic concepts are, however, no longer confined to such an intimate setting. Psychology has become pro-active, rapidly evolving into a tool for achieving self-fulfilment and other things through *change* – something anyone is able to undergo, given sufficient determination. However, the most profound development has been that it is no longer necessary to engage a psychotherapist in order to be introduced to contemporary ideas of self-fulfilment. A vast array of new conceptions, beliefs and assumptions concerning the human condition has been made ubiquitous, particularly through publishing, the media, and the idea of 'personal development' and 'self-improvement'.

As of the late 1960s, psychological concepts began to be misappropriated on a grand scale, for psychology was no longer merely restricted to getting rid of 'problems', rather, it began to concern itself with issues of greater happiness, 'self-fulfilment', 'self-esteem', and 'growth'. People began to expect to be taught 'how to feel good about themselves', how to be happy or happ*ier*. Contentment, accepting oneself and being true to oneself – states that few would normally be fortunate enough to experience in a lifetime – have, for many, become modest aspirations which have been superseded by the belief in various forms of growth, development and fulfilment. People have, of course, throughout history, adopted various ideologies, not to mention drugs, in expectation of a greater happiness. The difference is, however, the sheer pervasiveness, intensity and the context in which our current expectations occur. Religions have tended to hold out the promise of happiness *after* one has led an exemplary life helping others; the new psychology aims for a more swiftly acquired form of spiritual gratification.

Proponents of growth argue that having goals and aspirations is a positive thing, an extension of the value our society places upon 'developing skills', 'enhancing', 'optimising', *improving* performance in a general sense. The psychology currently on offer fits in rather neatly with the ethos of striving for excellence; it also happens to fill a spiritual void and meet a social and economic need. Whereas previously our expectations of self-fulfilment and how to experience it were formed primarily by our childhood experiences, our family's beliefs, values and aspirations, life events and spiritual frameworks, these now play second fiddle to the influence of society's obsession with betterment and achievement. All of this is perfectly reflected on a populist level as expressions such as 'count your blessings' or 'as you sow so shall you reap', have given way to more gracious transatlantic utterances such as 'Go For It!' and 'Be the best you can be.'

It may of course seem preferable to believe that one is impervious to the whims of psychological fashion. Such gullibility may be easily dismissed as something merely to be expected of self-indulgent therapy enthusiasts or of those who read *Cosmopolitan* – and believe it. However, it is quite clear that the new aspirations have permeated every echelon and corner of society in some way or other. Even Britain's Royal Family, who could easily afford to live in separate castles should their relationships falter, now have expectations of achieving 'fulfilling relationships'. While psychology's escape into the community has taken many entertaining forms – such as seeing one's father being caught up involuntarily in an impromptu spot of male bonding – there have been other ramifications which are far less agreeable.

The belief in personal growth and self-improvement reinforces a disapproval of oneself in favour of becoming a 'new person'. Moreover, self-improvement is not a harmless exercise in growth, it is too often a *rejection* of one's persona, an attack upon one's own identity, which itself is hard enough to understand before one begins to tamper with it. Such efforts can be counter-productive, merely adding more layers of self-deception to peel away when one is ultimately forced to confront the question which has become increasingly difficult to answer – 'Who am I?'

As if to add insult to injury, those who feel the need for self-improvement do so precisely because they feel dissatisfied with themselves, but by failing to realise the expected improvements or changes, they may instead experience yet a *further* sense of personal failure and dissatisfaction – a similar experience to a failed attempt at sticking to a diet. The cruellest irony is that the ideologies and strategies intended originally to help individuals lead happier, more fulfilled lives, have actually served to cause greater confusion and disillusionment, helping to create feelings of emotional entitlement which can never be realised. If, for example, one considers the way in which elements of reconstructive surgery have been misrepresented and promoted irresponsibly as cosmetic surgery, the misappropriation of psychology seems merely the cerebral end of this trend. Conspicuous consumption literally gone to the head.

The misappropriation of psychology is difficult to pin down as the 'articles' concerned are intangible. Without wanting to appear pedantic or petty, this process is facilitated by the public's ignorance of the distinction between professions described as 'counselling' or 'therapy' which require no qualifications – literally anyone can, and many do, describe themselves as a 'counsellor' or 'therapist' – and professions with an academic basis such as psychology and psychiatry or biology or neuro-physiology; indeed, it is against the law to refer to oneself as a psychologist or psychiatrist unless one has the relevant academic qualifications. It is the counsellors, therapists and management consultants who have exploited the ideas of the academics, and in turn, like Chinese Whispers, the media has exploited these already exploited concepts. Those with an academic background, on the whole, couldn't organise a nervous breakdown in a psychiatric hospital, let alone bring about the misappropriation of their own ideas.

2: New and Improved?

There was a time when self-improvement could be achieved through consuming tinned, green vegetables, and a certain maritime cartoon character was allowed to declare the sentiment 'I am what I am what I am what I am' – Olive Oyl wouldn't want him any other way. However, the way one conceptualises oneself has changed radically. The self seems to have been privatised and atomised. On the one hand, the self constitutes the uniqueness of the individual – the awareness we have of the distinction between oneself and others – while, at the same time, recent notions have considered the self as existing in a void. Once the self has been considered as a separate entity, it can be 'worked on'. This development is not surprising, for one can sense a feeling of malaise and despondency within our society, a sense of loss over the lack of large meaningful systems to account for everyday life and experience.

Religion and ideology have lost their mass appeal and now appear to be rather distant routes to salvation. At one time, Western societies could have seriously considered Marx's means of achieving the liberation of the individual through radical change *en masse*, or, for the more affluent clientele, the creation of a better society via the personal liberation of the individual as derived through Freud's *chaise longue*. It isn't necessarily that we are suddenly becoming emotional narcissists, rather, the focus on working upon the self is a symptom of our feeling that we have little personal authorship and influence on society. A response to feeling ineffectual, whereby working on the self becomes a solution in itself. There appears to be a greater trend toward living our emotional lives vicariously, not through

19

cheering on Popeye as he saves his sweetheart, but through the emotional lives of far less realistic celebrities who serve as a source of comfort to us, in that our own feelings somehow seem 'valid' because they have been experienced by someone with an Equity card. In a fame-literate, fragmented and ever self-alienating society, Britain's three prime-time long-running soap operas provide us with a type of global village of emotions – feelings by proxy – the chance to get in touch with someone else's emotions. Bet Lynch's, perhaps?

One aspect of society's current interest in psychology is the fact that we are now less tolerant of unhappiness or emotional distress. Consistent with its view of ageing skin, American culture has implied that pain too is almost optional, suffering is not inevitable. Western society, with its attendant consumerism, inculcates us with the belief that we can and *should* be happy: few people in adverts cry. Moreover, the American view of happiness is rather synthetic, based upon an inability to tolerate the full range of emotions. Those outside the US, however, may subscribe to a different definition: 'happiness is a failure to understand how bad things are.' While it is quite unnecessary to adopt a vale of tears stance, life *does* necessarily entail pain and sorrow. We learn by pain, as any infant can tell you, and the lessons we learn through this educational process are more likely to stay with us. Moreover, repression and misery have advantages for society. In Britain, traditionally, the Arts have been the only acceptable outlet for emotions, rather unfortunate for those who are repressed and miserable, but nevertheless enjoyable for the rest of us.

For many people, science has replaced religion as a more factual frame of reference in which to understand the world and our existence, and as psychology is considered a science, it is psychology that has provided a more pragmatic, spiritual frame of reference. The ascendancy of contemporary psychology to this status should prompt some critical retrospective look at previous frameworks. Platonic philosophy held that there was one true form for truth, one true form for beauty, etc. Physicist Danah Zohar observes: 'Christian thinking, like the Platonic philosophy with which it was so closely associated, is what we might describe as "top down". It starts with a unified vision of truth and imposes this on the world as a ready-made set of beliefs. The foundation of these beliefs is revelation and authority.'

Psychology, on the other hand, is appropriated in a way which avoids outright value judgements about behaviour through the use of 'relativism' when, of course, it is politically advisable. Much anti-social behaviour is often 'explained' and 'understood' as opposed to condemned as utterly unacceptable. Therefore, somewhat paradoxically, the image of psychology is thus seen as one which is happy to be propositional – defining certain forms of positive behaviour – whilst at the same time, opting out of judging other behaviour which may be politically sensitive.

Where psychology excels is in measuring and observing behaviour. If this were a pure process, one could rely upon this discipline as a trustworthy frame of spiritual reference. However, the human condition is often observed through tinted spectacles and the notion of 'measuring' human nature must prompt the question of precisely *what* one is going to measure and *how* one measures it. And then, of course, there is the question of interpreting one's results. Therefore, psychology should not be discredited, but the motivation and bias of many 'interpreters' should be more closely examined.

Much of the new, accessible psychology appears to hold out the opportunity for self-empowerment, encouraging individuals to get in touch with their inner sources of 'authority' and to take control of their lives. Yet no 'expert' can 'self-empower' someone else. Such a belief, while terribly appealing in many ways, rather insidiously promotes one's *disempowerment*. Coupled

21

with erroneous assumptions and fashionable ideas concerning human nature, this situation becomes a self-fulfilling prophecy. Current psychological philosophies which have mass appeal, appear in reality to assume a high degree of existing uniformity amongst the population which is why they assume they are relevant to everyone. Such approaches ignore diversity. One of the most unfortunate consequences of this is that, in pursuing such approaches, we may be distracted from acknowledging aspects of ourselves that do not conform and one may even imagine conformity where it doesn't actually exist. One may adhere to such an approach, deriving short-lived comfort from the belief that true growth is close at hand.

If one pauses to reflect upon what has actually happened, it becomes clear that psychology has been misused to nudge the individual toward greater conformity. 'Discover your true self', has been subtly extended to include '. . . and then change what you have found in order to improve it.' The modern emphasis on modifying character has overlooked the importance of simply coming to terms with oneself. Moreover, our culture has always thrived on diversity, not uniformity; there is no place for drip-dry personalities. There is a slight paradox in all of this, when on the one hand the discipline that has brought us such reassuring truisms such as 'every one of us is a unique and wonderful *individual*' is also making it known that *actually*, one could be even more wonderful and unique if one was more like 'this' or less like 'that'.

The most prolific populist example of empowering people on a mass level is quite reminiscent of that employed by American evangelists and their followers. A charismatic new breed who refer to themselves as 'personal development consultants', say enthusiastically: '*I* did it, so can *you*!' There are rallies, seminars, support groups, courses, books, cassettes and CDs to back up their main philosophy for changing in order to achieve one's goals. Such activities also help to cultivate a degree of idolatry for the personal development consultant . . . the new saviour. Britain had its first major taste of this when Mr Victor Kiam revealed 'I Liked It So Much – I Bought The Company!' At the moment, the most renowned exponent of this is the American, Anthony Robbins, who at the tender age of twenty five published his self-actualisation blockbuster *Unlimited Power*, which claims:

> Yes, you can do, have, achieve, and create anything you want out of life. Whatever you think, will be, your state of mind determines what you can and can't do . . . all successful results can be modelled and duplicated. Reprogram your mind in minutes to eliminate fears and phobias, dramatically improve your interpersonal relationships. Become a persuasive communicator and create instant rapport with anyone you meet. Use the success of others to remodel yourself. . . . It's the new science of personal achievement.

A variation on the theme of 'everyone can be President if they really want to'. It should, however, seem blatantly obvious that very few people can 'make it', in fact that is one of the reasons why the United States is so violent and why Britain is becoming more so. Self-improvement appears to be a contemporary manifestation of The American Dream. The important aspect of this new trend is that it is not in the slightest bit New Age – in fact, it is highly achievement-orientated, almost corporate in its approach. In an ironic twist of ideology, an indulgence once practised by radicals in beards and sandals has now been taken up by those within The System in order to 'achieve results' through this 'new science of personal achievement'.

One of the most erroneous propositions of recent times is that, to a large extent, we 'choose to feel' the way we do about certain events in our lives. Negative emotional responses are met with the explanation that it wasn't the person or the situation that caused your responses but *you* who chose to feel 'negative and destructive emotions' when you could instead have 'reframed' the scenario in a far more positive way. If, say, at a party, someone were to call you 'a nefarious little cunt', instead of viewing it as a humiliating and threatening public insult, you should look at it as a novel way of learning new permutations within the English language.

At the heart of self-improvement is the necessity for personal change. One is led to believe that change is *good* and that change is *possible*; however, both of these assumptions are highly questionable. It is difficult enough to change just our veneer, let alone our innermost characteristics. This is where the British class system provides us with a wonderful admonition of the inherent limitations of self-improvement. We readily accept that sending a cockney car mechanic to evening classes in elocution and etiquette is unlikely to transform him into a foolproof member of the middle classes. His boiler suit is not the only thing that would betray him, for no amount of personal tuition from Professor Higgins can erase his deeply ingrained social characteristics and mannerisms. 'You can't make a silk purse out of a sow's ear.' Yet when it comes to the promise of even deeper change through modern psychological 'techniques', we suspend our critical faculties. However, like the talent for playing a musical instrument or speaking a foreign language, the ability to change-by-numbers is a facility which most people *don't* possess and *cannot* cultivate. To lead people to believe otherwise is simply irresponsible. When considering other aspects of character, for instance, would it seem possible for a humourless person to cultivate a sense of humour?

There are some common techniques employed to help people believe in the accessibility of change. One major source of

24

deception involves leading us to believe that, by learning more about what makes us tick, we will naturally be able to 'work' on certain areas and therefore change them. A combination of misguided Californian optimism and commercial opportunism has taken things several stages further, to confuse, intentionally, the ability to *understand* oneself, with the ability to *change* not only behaviour but feelings and even personality.

There are a number of factors which have an enormous bearing on one's ability to make significant personal changes. These details are, however, studiously avoided by the advocates of change, and with good reason. Biology is rather an embarrassing inconvenience to the proponents of self-improvement, a subject viewed with disdain, for it runs in direct contradiction to many of the possibilities presented by 'change' psychology. A discipline which involves hard facts, elements of predetermination, and worst of all, limitations, is considered almost spiritually fascistic by those who hate facing reality . . . and dream weaving is, of course, a far more lucrative endeavour. Thus the prevailing attitude toward biological influences is to 'acknowledge and ignore'.

Expressions like 'you can't teach an old dog new tricks' do not feature highly within this psychology, because such ideas reek of 'ageism', and besides 'you're only as old as you feel'. Little consideration is given to the specific limitations that ageing places upon one's mind. For 'The Mind' is revered as an entity, quite distinct from anything as worldly as the brain. Rather, minds possess exciting libertarian qualities such as free will, while brains, with their grey matter, seem ever so constricting in comparison. Focusing upon brain structure and function is seen as somehow killing the mystery. Despite society's reluctance to accept the ageing process, and at the risk of falling prey to the adage 'shoot the messenger', it is necessary to rub one's wrinkled face in a few carefully chosen realities of ageing. The following may also serve as a vivid reminder of how youth can be wasted on the young.

The average man reaches his reproductive peak at about 18.5 years, has the capacity for peak physical fitness at about 25 years and after 30 years of age his body composition shifts from lean muscle to fat at a rate of about 1 per cent a year. What is most relevant to this discussion is the fact that the brain, like most other parts of the anatomy (with the possible exception of the waistline), shrinks with age. When considering the themes of 'learning', 'changing', 'growing' and 'developing', Patrick Rabbitt, Professor of Cognitive Gerontology (the study of the effects of ageing upon the mind) at Manchester University, has few reservations about being honest, stating, quite simply, that 'the brain rots.' While skills learned earlier in life may be retained into one's later years, they become, according to Professor Rabbitt, 'islands of competence in an ebbing sea of mediocrity'.

Moreover, brains do not wait until retirement age before they begin to deteriorate. Nor, for that matter, do many intellectual abilities, which grow very rapidly in childhood and slow down in the teens. It is the *young* who have the capacity to learn many languages, numerous musical instruments and to become far more computer literate, *not* adults. The young brain has a far greater degree of 'plasticity', brain cells form many more synapses (new connections) as it acquires new information. In fact, it is thought that there are *critical periods* in development when a child's brain is most plastic and ready to acquire some of the behaviour and emotional skills essential for optimal development later. During these periods both favourable and unfavourable circumstances have lasting and irreversible consequences. If the appropriate experiences do not occur during these windows of emotional and intellectual opportunity, then these can be learned later only with the greatest of difficulty, if at all. Between the ages of

5 and 11, for example, the ability to acquire language declines. After puberty, it is nearly impossible to learn to speak a foreign language without an accent.

Dramatic evidence of this is found in children who literally had no upbringing, locked in a room from a very early age without any contact with others. The well-known case of the American girl, 'Jeanie', sadly demonstrated that the huge scientific investment in teaching her to speak, led to little. Cases of children who were abandoned in the wild at birth and brought up by wolves (*feral children*), yet later discovered and introduced to civilisation, show that they never developed either. A number of such cases have served as celebrated works of art, for example François Truffaut's *L'Enfant Sauvage*, tells the true story of the late eighteenth century Dr Jean Itard who took in such a child – 'Victor'. Despite intensive exercises in vocalisation which even involved placing the boy's hands on people's throats to feel how the muscles help form sounds, the boy could not learn to speak. It appears that even when such feral children are drilled continually, while they may learn specific words, they cannot combine and structure language. They often display merely a form of mimicry known as *echolalia*. No amount of intense education could overcome the original deprivation they experienced. All of the special teaching and clinical professors in the world cannot teach these children to speak or respond in a functional way. Brain development is inextricably linked to our ability to learn and change. In other words, miss the boat, and you grow up emotionally illiterate. Romulus and Remus's wolf-mother obviously knew the importance of a good education.

People are quite happy to acknowledge genetics when the discussion is confined to characteristics such as eye colour or congenital deformities. However, once the conversation turns to the tremendous influence genes may have upon intellectual, emotional and sexual characteristics, public psychology becomes rather hard of hearing. For many people, the term *genes* means *limitations*, and limitations are unwelcome. For some time, genetics was essentially a derogatory term when used to help explain social behaviour. This was no doubt helped by its rather unfortunate association with eugenics and ethnic cleansing. As a result, the past fifty years have seen an excessive focus upon social factors such as the amount of love and attention a child receives, the social class and wealth of a child's parents, etc. The pendulum, however, is swinging.

There was a time when it was quite acceptable to maintain that intellectual aptitudes and limitations were, to a large extent, inherited. Then the 'right on' politics of the 1960s arrived and such ideas became terribly uncool. Academics were told to play down the influences of *nature* and focus instead upon things that could be more easily controlled (and changed) – *nurture*. For example, in the case of identical twins, who always develop from a single egg, they share precisely the same heredity; even when they are separated at birth and reared apart in different homes, their IQs are far closer than those of non-identical twins reared together.

Studies have moved on to look at the heritability of personality and emotional predisposition, with hundreds of twin studies suggesting a large genetic contribution to a wide variety of behaviour from shyness to being authoritarian. Contrary to being threatening, these new findings could actually make parenting a somewhat more relaxed affair. Professor Robert Plomin of the Centre for Social, Genetic and Development Psychiatry at the Maudsley Hospital, which is funded by the Medical Research Council, explains: 'Knowing that shyness has a large genetic element takes the pressure off the child being forced to "learn" to be sociable, while the parents don't have to worry whether they "caused" it, either by going out too much or too little. . . . Genetics can't determine values, but it is a perspective that concentrates on the individual. It could help to guide social policy. You could decide to put resources in to help those whose genes put them at a cognitive disadvantage, rather than penalising them.'

We are willing to accept that some psychiatric disorders such as manic depression can be inherited, but any suggestion that we are predisposed to be dour is met with great resistance. Personality characteristics such as shyness or a negative outlook can be predicted from the behaviour of small babies. Even at birth, investigators are finding, children vary in their emotional reactions to people and events, suggesting a hereditary contribution to temperament. Studies of children over a period of time by Harvard University psychologist, Jerome Kagan, show marked differences between those who are 'inhibited' − shy, quiet and socially withdrawn − and their more talkative, outgoing and sociable peers. Kagan has found that inhibited children have higher and more stable heart rates, react more to stress and may be more prone to depression and anxiety disorders later in life. We are, however, informed that even if we are born with a frown on our face, it can, of course, be 'worked on' and changed. Yet being constantly lectured about 'those who see a glass as half-full versus those who see it as half-empty' is enough to make one reach for the bottle.

There has never been much of a fuss made about the heritability of musical talent. An example is that of the Bach family, which produced more than 60 professional musicians. Similarly, most of us know people who, despite endless violin lessons, still sound like a squeaky door. Nevertheless, controversy has broken out within the British Psychological Society over the question 'is everyone musical?'. Several professors argue that any disparity in musical talent is due to social and motivational factors and opportunities for musical education as opposed to innate ability. Moreover, they believe that even *mentioning* the idea of musically gifted children will cause other, less gifted children to fail early and often, to avoid disappointment; a case of information creating a self-fulfilling prophecy. Fortunately, there are some, less affected psychologists, such as Professor John B. Davies: 'Given the middle-class liberalism that underlies much psychological theorising at the present time, it might seem reactionary to argue against notions which are egalitarian and which spring from the best of motives. But such a stance is not necessarily reactionary. Apparently liberal, appealing and moral notions sometimes contain the seeds of a kind of false consciousness which can manifest itself in unexpected and undesirable ways. . . . The fact that Linford Christie trains an awful lot in no way supports a theory that we can all potentially run 100 metres in under 10 seconds.' Those who find genetic predispositions somewhat hard to swallow may be interested to know that both Leonard Bernstein and Ira Gershwin grew up in pianoless households.

Even if one is intent on changing one's genetic dispositions, one must realise that the ability to *learn* is a facility which is also influenced not only by critical periods of development, but also by genetics.

While some may consider this as the 'glass as half-empty' view of human character, it is intended as a form of reassurance and relief. Many people do not have ideal childhoods and may end up with emotional 'short-comings'. While it is important to *acknowledge* that things might have turned out differently, efforts to rectify or recapture previous opportunities would, in many cases, be better spent on gaining a much deeper sense of self-knowledge. It is actually Popeye who seems to have things in perspective. Anyone who experiences self-acceptance is most fortunate.

Ultimately, change tends to occur either through catecholismic life events or through evolution. Moreover, change must come from *within*. The French anatomist Duchenne de Boulogne studied the distinction between the false, 'social' smile and the smile of true enjoyment, which he described as being 'put into play only by the sweet emotions of the soul.' Self-modification is often derived from the intellect and is nothing more than a form of echolalia (see p. 27).

So, one must ask, where did the influences which have helped us cultivate such a penchant for psychological mimicry originate?

3: California Dreaming

The Vienna of 1893 was not exactly what one would refer to as 'Surf City'. While Adolf Hitler embarked on his dysfunctional childhood upbringing, other Austrians were occupied mainly with making hot chocolate. Freud's neighbourhood wasn't oozing with the overwhelming opulence that characterised the better-known parts of Vienna; number 19, Bergasse, is plain drab and not really the kind of setting you would think inspiring enough to produce such supremely sexist observations and subsequent musings.

Jeffrey Masson, author of *Against Therapy*, is on the crest of the current fashion amongst liberal intellectuals to deride Freud as a phallo-centric misogynist. The discrediting of Freud has now become a small industry in itself with academic careers flourishing as a result. *Against Therapy* possesses the naivety of an undergraduate who, after studying history for three years, suddenly 'discovers' that democracy isn't perfect. Despite such lamentation, Freud has contributed tremendously to our understanding of the human condition. In particular, his recognition that unconscious needs and conflicts motivate much of our behaviour. Freud saw much of man's behaviour as being determined by innate instincts which are largely unconscious, rather than the rational reason the individual might give for his behaviour. One major psychology textbook describes Freud's view of human nature as '. . . essentially negative. Man is driven by the same basic instincts as animals and he is continually struggling against a society that stresses the control of these impulses.' To describe our similarity to animals as 'negative', is insulting to animals and

33

ignores the relative sophistication of their behaviour. What other species would grab a machine gun and mow down a restaurant full of its own kind, even though it has got a full stomach and its own centrally heated, fully carpeted nest? In the final analysis, Freud's way of conceptualising our personality structure actually seems rather useful as a shorthand, consisting of three major systems which interact to govern behaviour:

The id
The original source of personality present in the new-born infant consisting of everything inherited, including the instinctual drives. It is closely linked to the biological processes and provides the energy source for all three systems. The *id* seeks immediate gratification of primitive, pleasure-seeking impulses and unorganised instinctual impulses. Like the new-born infant, it endeavours to avoid pain and obtain pleasure regardless of any external considerations. Although the two other aspects to personality develop later (one hopes), the *id* remains with us always and constantly serves as a major force in our lives.

The ego
The controlling self that holds back the impulses of the *id* in the effort to delay gratification until it can be found in socially approved ways. The 'executive' of the personality, deciding what actions are appropriate and which *id* instincts will be satisfied and in what manner. It takes into account the implications of acting impulsively, being realistic and logical and planning how to achieve satisfaction. In many ways the *ego* is our 'self', the rational, reasoning part of our personality. The *ego* mediates between the demands of the *id*, the realities of the real world and the demands of the *super ego*.

The super ego
This corresponds closely to an uncompromising and punishing conscience based upon the values and morals of society. Punishment comes in the form of guilt. Its main functions are to inhibit the impulses of the *id* (particularly those that society prohibits, such as sex and aggression), to persuade the *ego* to substitute moralistic goals for realistic ones, and to strive for perfection. It is the manifestation of idealism and therefore often places unrealistic demands upon the individual. Popular with the Vatican.

As a rough guide to personality structure and dynamics, Freud's system works well. It is interesting to note, almost a century later, how Freud's three-tier structure of personality corresponds somewhat to the rough anatomical structure of the human brain, which consists of three evolutionary layers:

The primitive core
The lowest and oldest part of the brain from an evolutionary point of view which, in addition to regulating complex reflexes such as heart rate and respiration, also drives impulses for eating, sleeping, awareness, sexual gratification, pleasure and pain, fear, rage, submission and domination. This structure is common to all animals – the primitive core of a snake or a rat is exactly the same as that of man. It is hated by feminists.

The limbic system
The next evolutionary level up from the primitive core which is not found in organisms below mammals. It is interconnected to the primitive core and seems to programme the activities necessary to satisfy some of its basic impulses and emotional needs. The 'instinctive' activities of lower animals, such as feeding, mating, attacking or fleeing, appear to be governed by the limbic system.

The cerebral cortex

The most recent part of the brain to evolve. This is where all complex mental activity takes place. As we ascend up the scale toward the higher mammals, the amount of cerebral cortex relative to the amount of 'below stairs' type of brain tissue increases. The cortex has a powerful influence on a wide variety of physical and psychological functions ranging from language, music appreciation and logic to fantasy and dreaming. It also analyses incoming information. In essence, it modulates, thinks about and rationalises and most notably *inhibits* signals from the limbic system and primitive core.

The psychology that emanated from America in the 1960s had little in common with its European predecessors. This is hardly surprising when one considers the history of the United States, a country started, and developed, by a gene pool of dynamic, adventurous people looking for a new life in a new world. This is reflected in the Western genre which epitomises the proclivity to forge new frontiers.

California, the final frontier, is somewhat different from Vienna. Californians also tend to waltz – but prefer to do this on roller skates. It provides the ultimate in 'go west' psychology and even one's surname may be found to inadvertently reflect the mood of the state. I recently came across an article by a certain San Franciscan named Dan Joy 'specialising in consciousness change'. . . . Humanistic psychology couldn't be further removed from psychoanalysis. Often referred to as the 'human potentialist movement', it encompasses a number of theories that share a common emphasis on man's potential for self-direction and freedom of choice, the movement which put the *self* into self-improvement. It focuses upon the individual's subjective conscious experiences. Individuals are free to *choose* and determine their actions. This view of man developed from the ideas of existential philosophers such as Kierkegaard, Nietzsche and Sartre, emphasising those 'human' qualities that distinguish man from animals; primarily free will and the drive toward fulfilling potential. Rather than viewing man as being acted on by forces *outside* of his control, he is instead considered an 'actor' capable of controlling his own destiny and changing the world around him.

Psychoanalytic conceptions of human nature are rejected as being too mechanistic, portraying people as creatures (animals!) helplessly buffeted about by internal instincts. Humanistic psychology stresses our positive nature, our push toward growth and self-actualisation; all biological needs are subservient to this. Humanistic psychology states that people have an ability to shape their own destiny, to chart and follow their own course of action, and that any biological instinctive, or environmental influences can be overcome. Therefore our *real* innate impulses *don't* involve fertilising hundreds of women with big bosoms or gorging ourselves on chocolate, but are directed towards growth – chaste greetings and passionate handshakes after completing a course in vegan cooking. When aware of the choices, it is argued, individuals have both the ability and the motivation to change in a positive direction.

This is a startling departure in both theory and practice from psychoanalysis where the therapist 'analysed' the patient's history to arrive at the problem. Humanistic psychology looks to the future rather than factors from the past which influence behaviour, such as genetics and early childhood experiences.

Abraham Maslow was a major figure in the Human Potentialist Movement. As the author of such works as *Self-Actualisation and Beyond*, Maslow looked at the human condition from the cerebral cortex down. 'Self-actualisation' meant the 'development of full individuality, with all parts of the personality in harmony'. Unlike Freud, who based his ideas essentially upon 'losers',

Maslow's ideas were based upon 'winners', eminent historical figures whom he considered to be 'self-actualisers' – men and women who had made extraordinary use of their full potential. Such figures included Albert Einstein, Abraham Lincoln and William James – a veritable Celebrity Squares of high achievers. After studying their lives, he arrived at a composite picture of a 'self-actualiser', along with a list of behaviours that could lead to 'self-actualisation', so we can emulate the more beneficial thought processes of the rich and famous and be successful ourselves. It is, however, important to ask whether such eminent public figures, deemed 'self-actualisers' in terms of their professional achievement, have much to show us about other areas of the human condition. For example, eminent 'self-actualisers' such as Abraham Lincoln and Eleanor Roosevelt, best known for their great concern for human welfare, did *not* seem to have 'self-actualised' within their own family relationships.

Returning to the three-tier structure of the human brain, it would appear that while Freud had a healthy regard for the primitive core which drives basic urges, human potentialists prefer to play down this bargain-basement of cheap impulses, choosing to travel two storeys higher in order to focus on the freedom of choice and rational thought afforded by the cerebral cortex. This upper echelon exudes qualities such as 'self-determination', 'choice', 'options', 'change' and 'being in control', whilst below-stairs lurk beastly inclinations, deference, submission, helplessness and controlling mercurial influences. Those interested in self-improvement, political correctness and social engineering see the cerebral cortex as the repository of computer software, endlessly up-dated with new programs according to the dictates of fashion. For the cerebral cortex represents human virtues such as parity and dignity regarded as being at odds with biological accounts of our behaviour. Yet by discounting this part of our make-up we deny the most fundamental part of human existence.

Author Adam Phillips, a child psychotherapist, writes of the misappropriation of Freud's ideas by successive generations of psychoanalysts. Freud's view of the human condition is seen as consisting of complex motives, mixed feelings and always being in two minds. As reviewer, Roy Porter, states: 'Being human was to be haunted by memory and desire and entangled in webs of forgetting and remembering; being conscious was not to know what one wanted or to want what one knew. Phillips' Freud is thus the supreme ironist, an artist ever alert to, and often amused by, the knotted contrariness of the human condition.' However, contrariness is not what the market demands, for shades of grey do not appear on modern society's colour chart of the human condition.

Therefore, it wouldn't take Saatchi & Saatchi to help one decide which school of thought is more presentable. Given the choice between the Freud 'Account' or the humanistic 'Account', it is obvious which one they would prefer to handle. Humanistic psychology is immensely appealing, a bit like the 'Classless Society', and comes fully equipped with its own advertising slogans. A copywriter couldn't ask for better raw materials than 'choice', 'being in control', 'freedom' and 'change'. Humanistic psychology seems so much more democratic than its authoritarian alternative. One can now begin to see why, with the right commercial acumen, it can be served up not only as a therapy but as a philosophy now available on CD, video and in all good bookshops. However, like too much democracy, placing so much choice and responsibility upon the individual can be insidiously oppressive.

Furthermore, the Sixties generation has finally come of age and is now running The System (and probably Saatchi & Saatchi). Those who were most in tune with the Sixties *Zeitgeist* have found their way into media, advertising and marketing and they have brought with them their perceptions of the 'self'. The writer, Bryan Appleyard, observes:

> To be young, male and groovy in the Sixties was to be possessed by a romantic intellectual error that has clung to the 20th century like a cheap suit. This is the belief that the self is a pure, pre-social entity, which life, society and culture distort and sully. This belief underpins . . . the entire growth, relationship and self-help industry, with its emphasis on unveiling the true self or the child within . . . The belief is an error because the very idea of a pre-social self is almost entirely incoherent, but it was an error whose time had come.

In questioning and rejecting the existing beliefs, many babies were thrown out with the bath water. Bernard Leach, for instance, in his 1968 Reith Lectures, declared that 'the family, with its narrow secrets and tawdry privacy, is the source of all our discontents'. Ironically, more than a quarter of a century later we find The Year of The Family. A jaundiced view of the family, combined with the demise of political or religious solutions to the human condition, turned the spotlight to the innocence of the true, liberated self where 'individuality' and 'inner freedom' reside. However, in order to reconcile former anti-Establishment sentiments with the realisation that, now, one *is* The Establishment, what better way to overcome such disparities than to use selectively many of the Sixties slogans to drive The System?

These 'baby-boomers' also grew up in a youth-obsessed time possessing greater affluence and technologies than ever before. The constraints acknowledged by their parents were swept aside and there seemed to be an approach, a technique, a solution to almost any of life's problems. However, more recently, Erica

Jong's autobiography, *Fear of Fifty*, has heralded this generation's sudden awareness of their own mortality: the generation who, in their enthusiasm for self-improvement, forgot to deal with the rather bothersome issues of ageing and dying. Death seemed almost optional and, given the title of one of the most successful popular health books of the moment, *Ageless Body – Timeless Mind*, to some it still is. Written by a well-known doctor who was recently appointed by the prestigious National Institutes of Health to one of its medical panels, and was Chief of Staff at the New England Memorial Hospital, the book's jacket proposes an 'Alternative To Growing Old', while the inside sleeve continues:

> . . . the effects of ageing are largely preventable. By intervening at the level where belief becomes biology, we can achieve our unbounded potential . . . gives readers tools to create new perceptions of ageing . . . we can take control of the way we age.'

Such literary efforts continue to feed the desperate beliefs of the generation that thought they could 'do what you wanna do, be what you wanna be' as an alternative to finding themselves in a state described by W.B. Yeats as 'sick with desire/And fastened to a dying animal'. As Professor Patrick Rabbitt observes: 'They are growing old disgracefully; they hate it. They were brought up with the idea that they can cure anything with jogging and other violent and harmful pursuits.'

It is therefore clear that in the same way that art is a reflection of the culture, era and even the weather conditions in which it develops, psychology is subject to its surroundings. During Freud's day, Middle European countries were limited by characteristics such as class systems; their borders consisted of irregular-shaped boundaries borne of tribal feuds down the centuries. They had traditions and they had history. In contrast, California's borders are virtually straight lines drawn with a ruler. With an abundance of sunshine, new insights and new beginnings just around the corner, it is hardly surprising that the *ego* and surfing flourished at the expense of the *id*. A lack of tradition and continuity is a fertile breeding ground for ever-changing psychological trends.

Ideas from therapy have therefore, in a way, become the handmaiden of our society's liberal democratic assumptions and romantic belief in the possibility of almost limitless self-improvement. Ironically, however, while psychotherapy was once a treatment, it has now become pro-active. Enticing people to self-improve has become an integral part of any self-respecting Western economy.

One can now begin to see how psychology has not only been absorbed by, but now helps drive the system. It is the Humanistic Movement which has been taken to heart and, while it has been diluted, it has become deeply ingrained in our culture. For surf-psychology has swept over institutions involved in everything from marriage guidance counselling to education and government policy. Even the emergence of political correctness was underpinned by such manufactured conceptions of human nature.

While contemporary psychology is perceived as a tolerant means to self-understanding, it is far from judgement-free. A glance at our recent past quickly reveals that therapists once viewed masturbation as a sick practice which **compromised** the Nation's eye-sight. Women with pre-menstrual syndrome were, until recently, sent to therapists for their 'emotional problems'. Only thirty years ago, homosexuality was 'cured' by electric-shock therapy which itself was preceded by psychosurgery. Psychology merely reflects the liberal consensus at any one time.

CALIFORNIA DREAMING

Psychology's prevailing 'wisdom' which guides our thought-processes involves egalitarian truisms such as: 'you can't generalise about people' and 'you shouldn't stereotype people.' These are the more contemporary manifestations of the Woodstock generation's expression, 'Hey, don't put me in a bag, man.' Psychology has no time for stereotyping and generalising because such preconceptions serve as psychological obstacles to *Change*. They smack of confines and limits. Psychology textbooks still attempt to dissuade would-be undergraduates from researching the validity of the 'wrong' sort of stereotypes for fear of opening a Pandora's box of 'isms'. For example, British psychologist N.J. Mackintosh believes: 'The possibility that there might be differences for IQ between different social or ethnic groups is usually thought to be a question of considerable social significance. It is certainly one which can be made by people of ill will. But it is not a question of any great scientific interest.'

The British Psychological Society has recently expressed great concern about stereotypes. A study of young offenders by Dr David Farrington concluded that a tattoo 'practically amounts to a badge of criminal tendencies as easy for the police to read as barcoding', and 'almost half of young offenders surveyed have tattoos'. 'Sensitive' psychologists were up in arms. Dr George Sik, in *The Psychologist*, wrote, 'over half of those surveyed *didn't* have tattoos . . . It makes psychologists look guilty of unforgivable levels of stereotyping. We must make sure the right message gets across.' However, as the American, Dr Lawrence Littig, pointed out, if 'fifty per cent of those arrested in that population are tattooed, then I would consider tattooing as a rather remarkably reliable indicator of criminal tendencies, probably much superior to any psychological tool in use today.' A picture is worth a thousand words.

If 'concerned' psychologists are interested in avoiding stereotyping, perhaps they would like to phase out comedy, an art form which is highly dependent upon stereotypes. Anyone who has stayed in a seaside hotel will know that Basil Fawlty was not conjured out of thin air, and anyone who has walked along London's Old Compton Street will know that Julian Clary is by no means unique. Woody Allen has packaged his large nose and other cultural characteristics to great effect, whilst street-ethnic Eddie Murphy is hardly likely to have based his characters on the Amish. The bigoted character Alf Garnett, upon which America's Archie Bunker was based, is one of many other examples. Alf's creator, Johnny Speight, believes: 'I never created Alf Garnett, society created him. . . . Politically correct people sweep things under the carpet, they live in a fictional world in which we should all love our neighbours. I think we should be wary of them; they might be burying bodies in the garden for all I know.' Warren Mitchell, who plays Alf, adds: 'I don't think politically correct people can see the joke.' Of course they can't, Mr Mitchell; like many psychologists, *not* having a sense of humour is a prerequisite to the job. John Cleese is somewhat concerned about this state of affairs and so, in an unlikely marriage, the Comedy Store teamed up with the Freud Museum to host a conference on humour and psychoanalysis. Stand-up therapists are still waiting for the phone to ring.

The concern over stereotypes and generalisations has been successful in making the audience in *Question Time* nod its collective head in hypocritical agreement when one of the panellists makes some utopian utterance in disapproval of sexual or racial stereotypes and generalisations about the working class or homosexuals. This benevolence is of course good for cultivating a re-electable image amongst the strata of the electorate who isn't watching female kick-boxing on the other side. We at least now feel ambivalent about openly stereotyping or generalising.

To persuade the population to cast off one of the most basic of psychological coping mechanisms is a gross abuse of contemporary psychological thinking. Generalising and stereotyping are absolutely essential to our ability to make sense of the world. We can only function *with* pre-conceptions or the world would appear a random, chaotic mess which would drive one quite mad. We tend to attribute characteristics to people based upon first impressions, e.g. colour, social class, sexual orientation, age and weight. Why shouldn't we? We need a template from which to work. Moreover, most people are simply crying out to be stereotyped. City types are partial to the grey suit to prove their devotion to the decimal point, while active gays present themselves in a completely different way which transmits their availability – at short notice. Grey-suited gays have a problem on their hands. And ignoring stereotypes can take all the fun out of modern, urban living . . .

A sultry evening, July 1993. A 35-year-old female BBC television director stands on the platform at Goldhawk Road tube station in London's Shepherd's Bush area. As she finishes her conversation on her mobile telephone, she notices two young black men replete in regulation street iconography – trainers, baseball caps worn backwards, baggy jeans, Tysonesque haircuts – evidently their role models did not include Sidney Poitier or Nelson Mandela. Her immediate *instinct* was to fold her phone and return it safely to her inside coat pocket. However, being white, middle class and of course feeling guilty for being so, she hesitates on jumping to rash conclusions based upon such trivial considerations as colour, dress sense, social class and a lurching, Neanderthal way of walking which was not exactly inspired by the *Alexander Technique*. She overrides her instinct and sits down on the bench, relaxed and trusting, the phone still in her hand. The two gentlemen saunter over and, sitting either side of her, engage her in an exchange of pleasantries, showing a keen interest in her telephone: 'what brand you got?'; 'what batt'ries does it use?'; 'where der the batt'ries go?'; 'what's the security code?', etc. She wrestles with her conscience: 'you can't generalise about people'; 'you shouldn't stereotype people'; 'hey, don't put them in a bag, man' – versus her true feelings: 'Oh my god! *He* isn't Sidney Poitier and *he* certainly isn't Nelson Mandela – actually, *they*'re two ethnically challenged criminals!!!!!' These two ethnically challenged individuals of course have no qualms about jumping to the rash but correct conclusion that this white, middle class, professional stereotype is compelled to be an Equal Opportunity victim. And so they dutifully obliged her by wresting the telephone from her hand and running off.

By the way, some schools in the United States are banning the sort of clothes which teachers associate with crime: baggy jeans, baseball caps, bandannas and football jackets. And even the eminent black civil rights activist, Jesse Jackson, is partial to stereotyping when he confessed publicly in the Autumn of 1993, 'There is nothing more painful to me at this stage in my life, than to walk down the street and hear footsteps and start thinking about robbery – then look around and see someone white and feel relieved.'

Legacies from humanistic psychology go further to misinform the public in order to prevent the victimisation of another minority group: those with a 'sexual preference' for their own gender. The Government's Health Education Authority book *Your Pocket Guide to Sex* is intended to empower the public to take charge of their own sex lives and to raise Britain's sexual self-esteem, being promoted as 'honest and packed with facts'. Hardly . . .

In discussing sexual orientation, the book states that 'sexuality is an ever-changing thing' and goes on to cite an out-dated study by Alfred Kinsey, *Sexual Behaviour in the Human Male*:

Not all things are black and all white, for nature rarely deals with discrete categories. Only the human mind invents categories and tries to force facts into separate pigeon holes. The living world is a continuum in each and every one of its aspects.

The HEA states:

As in all areas of human activity, people want to make rules about sexuality. The truth is there are no rules. . . . Because we live in a predominantly heterosexual society . . . there's a risk that homosexual feelings get thought of as . . . abnormal.'

In point of fact, male homosexuality *is* 'abnormal', as is being left-handed. Things *are* terribly black and white and there *are* definite natural rules; nature *does* deal in discrete categories. Outside of the creative ghettos of London's fashionable West End, there is no evidence that more than a tiny minority of men are homosexual or bisexual. However, female homo/bi-sexuality appears to be a less clear-cut issue for a number of reasons. To begin with, female sexuality is markedly different from that of males (see Chapters 4 and 5). Women are also encouraged to be far more tactile and so the dividing line between lesbianism and close friendship is more difficult to detect from the outside than it would be in the case of men. Some women appear to have the facility to make a 'political' decision to be gay, possibly as the result of bad experiences with men. Novelist Joanna Briscoe relishes this state of affairs, expressing the 'right' views on the subject: 'The great sexual divide has never been gauzier. You can see it on the club scene. Straight clubs have become a little gay, gay clubs a little straight. There's plenty between two extremes of the sexual scale – exclusive homosexuality and exclusive heterosexuality.'

This line of thought has been extended to sexuality in general. While the notion of a continuum is an attractive egalitarian way of looking at our sexual orientation, it is intended to be misleading. It implies an 'even spread' of sexual orientation, with all shades being equally represented, for a continuum is seen as a line with two opposing positions, one at either end:

Heterosexuality — — — — — — — — — — — — — — — *Homosexuality*

the middle presumably representing bi-sexuality. And such an analogy therefore implies that pure heterosexuality is one extreme end of the scale, insinuating that these people have *chosen* to ignore the small part of their persona which, in a more tolerant society, would have enabled them to enjoy their dormant homosexual side. Wishful thinking: male homosexuality is neither chosen nor changeable and most men are straight. Section 28 is therefore an utterly unnecessary piece of legislation.

In yet another attempt to dissuade us from generalising, the received wisdom on sexual orientation goes further to claim that homosexuals are no different from heterosexuals except for in what they get up to in the bedroom; 'remember we're all just people'. What an odd thing to believe. For while attempting to provide comfort to an oppressed minority group by making them appear like everybody else, this patronising view actually displays a remarkable lack of tolerance toward diversity. It denies many homosexuals their identity. Homosexuals are not the same as heterosexuals and this is rather fortunate. It is hardly sheer coincidence that gays have traditionally contributed immensely to our culture, particularly within the Arts. One's sexual orientation says *everything* about the way one conceptualises the world. A man possessing the stereotypical male characteristics of assertiveness, aggressiveness, drive, compulsion, competitiveness, coupled with 'female' qualities, is bound to produce unique insights and perspectives otherwise unavailable to the majority.

Another 'protected species' is the working class. Social class should be of immense importance to *all* psychologists interested in understanding or changing the human condition, and thus one would have thought a highly relevant factor in self-improvement. However, it has been predictably swept under the rug in order to avoid what they see as yet another limitation. After all, biology and genetics are limiting enough without have to contend with the tugging of forelocks. Psychologists are reluctant to acknowledge general characteristics about a specific social sector, as in the case with ethnic minority groups and homosexuals. Part of the explanation for this omission may lie in the fact that Britain is influenced by American psychology which emanates from a young culture without a deeply rooted class system. In any event, American psychologists would naively confer upon themselves the ability to help one transcend one's class constraints. A veritable army of Rex Harrisons.

Professor Michael Argyle in his book *The Psychology of Social Class*, based upon long-term studies of class differences, has concluded: 'Most aspects of human well-being are closely linked to social class in some way. Plans to enhance human happiness and well-being must take this into account.' When researching happiness, he states: 'The main result is clear: people of higher social class are somewhat happier . . . It may be because a middle-class life provides more joyful experiences.' Class differences in personality were also found: 'Middle-class people tend to be more inner-directed and to have stronger achievement motivation, longer-term goals; working-class individuals tend to be more aggressive and authoritarian.' Moreover, the starting point for any attempt to achieve happiness through self-improvement differs between classes. 'There are extensive class differences in mental health . . . Working-class people are

49

also more vulnerable to stress because of lower levels of internal control, lower self-esteem and less effective styles of coping.' Professor Argyle believes that much of this is to do with 'rigid and punitive styles of child-rearing', which also helps explain the differences in 'aggressiveness, crime and authoritarianism.'

Yet, like many psychologists, Professor Argyle believes that 'this is a source of behaviour which is capable of modification . . . and this could be enhanced by better socialisation.' However, returning to the concept of critical periods in development, is it really possible to redress such fundamental deficiencies by implementing such well-intentioned panaceas at a much later stage?

Interesting ideas from humanistic psychology have also made their way into another world-class Centre of Excellence – Rugby, headquarters of RELATE, formerly known as the Marriage Guidance Council. RELATE is perceived by most as an Establishment organisation with royal backing, which exists to provide impartial help to those experiencing difficulty within their relationships. RELATE describes itself as offering 'relationship and sexual counselling for couples and individuals'. Unlike 'therapy', the term 'counselling' has a less intimidating image, a temporary helping hand for a specific type of problem. Counsellors prefer to see themselves as having fewer dogmatic ideas about how the human mind works. Unlike Freudians, Jungians or Gestaltists, such services appear to be 'culture-free' in their approach to the human condition. RELATE sees itself as just 'being there', on the side of the person in need, without any pre-conceptions or value judgements. This is a terribly self-delusionary stance to adopt.

RELATE have now gone from responding to marital difficulties to becoming pro-active by reaching out to help people *improve* their existing relationships. Their manifesto is revealed in the recent publication of three of their books, *The RELATE Guide to Better Relationships, The RELATE Guide to Sex in Loving Relationships* and, for those whose relationships were neither better nor loving, *The RELATE Guide to Starting Again*. The titles are rather telling in themselves. The term 'guide' implies a received wisdom which lies within the pages ready and waiting to be imparted to the great uninformed. The term 'better' brings with it the prospect of 'tinkering' with one's relationship, i.e. actively choosing to change the dynamics of something quite amorphous – improving it.

Further clues as to RELATE's links with American 'change' psychology are to be found on the back covers. *The RELATE Guide to Sex in Loving Relationships* states:

As RELATE knows from over fifty years of working with couples, you can make a bad sex life good, and a good sex life even better. This book shows you how to . . . create a sex life that is tailor-made for your relationship alone. Step-by-step [it] shows you how to . . . draw up your own 'better sex' plan.

While the cover of *The RELATE Guide to Better Relationships* reads like an ad for a new and improved soap powder:

Few things in life cause more distress than when problems develop and communication between partners breaks down . . . no-one knows better than RELATE how to overcome difficulties and, in doing so, create a good and lasting relationship. Now, For The First Time . . . learn how to talk, listen – and hear, deepen your love through tackling problems together, improve your sex life.

The tone and general message reduce relationships and sex into manageable components, relegating them to the level of Delia Smith's recipes. Expressions such as 'tailor-made', 'draw up

51

your own better sex plan', 'you can make', 'you can create', 'step-by-step', 'NOW FOR THE FIRST TIME', and 'deepen your love' exemplify the emphasis on *change, improvement, betterment*.

Whether one is suffering mid-mugging guilt on a station platform or rowing in Rugby, one's reactions are ultimately bound to be influenced by distorted and misappropriated elements of psychology. The introduction of such notions has also failed to take into account profound national differences between Britain and America. The strong emphasis on directness and honesty has ignored the British reliance on nuance, non-verbal communication and apologetic behaviour.

National differences are not the only differences that have been ignored by contemporary psychology.

4: Ignoring Janet and John

It is extraordinary and remarkably sad that it still seems necessary to allocate an entire chapter to the blatantly obvious; that men and women are profoundly different. Artists of all talents have always acknowledged, and often lamented, the stark differences between men and women. In fact, such differences have provided the basis for the greatest works of art.

Hollywood, whilst not exactly renowned for its concern with producing great works of art, has not been blind to such gender differences – especially when it comes down to making money. Hollywood has always made 'girl movies' and 'boy movies'. In the old days the guiding principle seemed to be that if a man and a woman were in a room together and they kissed, it was a 'girl movie'. If he shot her, it was a 'boy movie'. Nowadays, of course, things are a bit more complex, as one seems to find movies where they kiss, then she shoots him. Even more recently, there are some clear examples of 'boy movies' and 'girl movies': *The Terminator* and *Dirty Harry* films as opposed to *Ghost* or *Truly, Madly, Deeply*. Hollywood executives believe that, in order for a film to make real money, it must appeal to both sexes. However, men often have difficulty enjoying 'women's movies' which tend to rely more upon dialogue, emotion and character development. 'Girls' movies' tend to explore the person experiencing the pain, whereas 'boys' movies' are more likely to explore the inflicting of it. The producer of the quaint *Die Hard* and *Lethal Weapon* series, Joel 'Sensitive' Silver, is widely quoted as saying: 'Women in my films are either naked or dead.' However, events seem to have overtaken him, as it would now appear that women are expected to possess both qualities to sell a film. Moreover, the big blockbuster action films do not appear particularly concerned about romance, or even sex for that matter – unless, of course, it's rape.

While differences between men and women have been acknowledged, what is still being disputed is the *basis* of these differences and, more importantly, whether they can be *changed* or overcome. Gender differences are played down and, in many cases, completely ignored by psychology, as they represent yet another obstacle to the path of change, not to mention yet another stereotype to overcome. People have been endlessly encouraged to believe that by behaving in a way which is more acceptable to the opposite gender, they would be brought closer together; unfortunately, the equality, friendship and understanding so eagerly awaited, seem to have been strangely evasive.

The prevalence of platonic relationships between men and women has, however, increased. Much of this is evolutionary, the result of women moving into the world of work and having to liaise with men. In addition to the laudable benefit of creating a more cohesive society, this development has provided the genders with an invaluable insight into how their counterpart's mind works, and such information can, with luck, contribute to a better understanding of one another. For example, those who have grown up in single-sex schools and those with no siblings of the opposite sex may have little opportunity to experience how the other half lives.

Through exposure to misinformation about the genders and their interaction, people's expectations have been cruelly raised and the gap between expectation and reality has become even wider. Gender stereotypes are immensely important and their erosion has been highly detrimental to relationships, creating in many cases deep and unnecessary anger and frustration. Predictably, American psychologists have observed this growing disenchantment, referring to it as 'Gender Rage', the growing disappointment couples feel when reality doesn't live up to expectations. If men and women feel enraged, perhaps they should be directing their wrath toward those who have attempted to misdirect and deny them their very essence.

Psychology seems to support the idea of controlled androgyny: a more extreme version of what was previously thought of as civilising one's prospective partner, i.e. 'smoothing over the rough edges'. Contemporary thought has promoted the idea that people can and should be lovers, friends, partners, soul mates and 'co-parents' within one relationship. The means of achieving this are by encouraging the genders (particularly men) to be more alike. This idea of convergence of the sexes does, upon first inspection, seem eminently sensible – like two competing organisations amalgamating in order to increase profitability. Separatism, the traditional inclination of males and females to pursue parallel courses, has been actively discouraged and is seen by many as obstructing the creation of a more harmonious and gratifying form of co-existence. It is, however, sadly ironic, that while men and women in general have come to appreciate each other's finer points, becoming friends, partners and 'amigos', that sense of 'otherness' which is vital for igniting sexual attraction is at risk from an outbreak of chronic mutual respect. When it comes to the intractable problems inherent in the relationship between men and women, it would seem more advisable to seek counsel from classic songwriters rather than psychologists:

> *The broken dates*
> *The endless waits*
> *The lovely loving and the hateful hates*
> *The conversations with the flying plates*
> *I wish I were in love again*

(Rogers & Hart)

In the same way that the differences in body shape serve as an attractant to the opposite sex, so too does the general difference in temperament. Being encouraged to meet half-way couldn't be a better form of natural contraception.

The new sexual agenda does not, unfortunately, sit well with what is both commonly observed and what is borne out of research. Women often appear to want a neat combination of mutually exclusive qualities. Even women of high professional status and income claim they desire men with even higher income and status. Women in general want a man high in both caring and cash – everything a girl needs for a well-balanced life. However, the qualities necessary to go out and accumulate the desired cash do not exactly go hand-in-hand with compassion.

This paradox is not the sole preserve of the ordinary person. January 1994, Prince Charles is visiting Australia. A gunman lunges from the crowd firing blanks at him. Charles seems somewhat oblivious to the goings-on which is all over in a matter of seconds. The headlines praise Charles for his self-control whilst 'in the line of fire'; *The Times* declares: 'Prince of Wales "Cool as a Cucumber" ' and the nation agrees that this is exemplary behaviour fit for a king. The same nation and media which so disapproved of the same remoteness and coolness he displayed as a husband and father. Even expectations of the Royal Family have been irreversibly changed by the 'new parenthood' which has been promoted by contemporary psychology. Britain felt that it was desirable, even for posh papas, to be warm, sensitive and attentive to their significant other partners and offspring alike. The fact that the years spent at public school (a world where bullying and buggery appear to take precedence over poetry and pottery), do not tend to cultivate an appreciation of qualities such as caring, sharing and support, didn't seem to concern the public which, by that time, had itself been exposed to new ideas about relationships and parenting. This conflict of expectations epitomises the competing demands placed upon the individual in modern relationships – demands which have been encouraged by politically desirable ideas and images, all publicly underpinned by psychology.

Although it may seem trite, it is nevertheless true that the issue of gender differences has been managed by a small number of highly unrepresentative individuals whose influential views often serve as contemporary examples of the sort of highly evolved lifestyles and relationships that are currently on offer to the sexes. While great time and emotional energy is now being directed at bridging the gender gap and enabling couples in modern society to cope with unrealistic expectations about respective partners, it may prove much more therapeutic to merely seek revenge on those responsible for the long-standing campaign of misinformation. Empowering oneself may ultimately be achieved through disempowering the influential. Embarking upon a witchhunt can be highly recommended as a remedy for an acute case of Gender Rage.

In launching the search for the perpetrators and the perpetuators, the media, in all its various forms, is a source of rich pickings. A vast number of magazine and book editors as well as television and radio producers are women, and many, if not most, of the positions below them are also filled by women. This is neither surprising nor in any way unfair, as women excel at reading people's needs, and responding and communicating to them. The media is not a sympathetic place, and the breed of women who succeed within this jungle are hardly representative (nor particularly sympathetic). However, many of them don't quite see it that way. It appears they see themselves as representing some form of high point on the socio-economic evolutionary scale, and feel that other women might like to experience second-hand what they have been 'fortunate enough' to see from their 'vantage' point. One must bear in mind that these are the same women who ushered in and promoted the unrealistic images of the female body which have contributed to so much dissatisfaction, self-loathing, anorexia and death. After attempting to engineer a trend toward physical androgyny, they have more recently directed their efforts toward creating a greater similarity between men and women in areas emotional and behavioural – with consequences which are just as disastrous. In some strange way, this has been considered a move toward 'parity'.

Such media hybrids have played the 'sisterhood' card, feigning camaraderie and a greater sororal link with women in general – under false pretences. An organisation called Women in Journalism has recently been formed by 'twenty top women journalists'. Its stated aims are 'to promote the interests of women and to help them get better pay and better jobs.' The formation of Women in Journalism (WIJ) was in response to a growing resentment concerning the inability of women 'to break through the glass ceiling' and attain powerful positions within the media. Ironically, one of WIJ's founders, Amanda Platell, when taking up her position as editorial manager at the *Daily Mirror* in 1993, created 'a new culture' by firing journalists including lots of first-class women journalists such as the crime correspondent, film critic, TV writer, fashion editor and graphics artist etc etc. A strange way of promoting the interests of women. And the camaraderie gets even better. The WIJ's founding 'Chairwoman', Eve Pollard, was a former editor of the *Sunday Express*. *Private Eye* reported that

> Other women who are unlikely to join Women in Journalism are Gill Morgan, Jane Owen, Sophie Chairmier, Ruth Chatto, Jill Crawshaw, Elizabeth Grice, Sophie Grigson, Aileen O'Brien, Diane Spencer, Mary Wilson, Daphne Broadhead, Aggie Mackenzie. All have worked for the *Sunday Express* and

felt the tender touch of the editor there, Women in Journalism founder Eve Pollard. All were sacked, driven from their jobs or forced to resign . . . by one of the few women who had broken the glass ceiling into a top job.

It is also somewhat illuminating to hear journalist Susan Crosland's view of such great female empathy, from the inside:

> . . . power women have abandoned Sisterhood for selfishness . . . camaraderie among women seems to falter once they are well up the ladder. Indeed, as a journalist, when you are first shown to your desk in the newsroom, you sense a wariness among women already established there. For each additional woman reduces the novelty power of her sisters. She has good reason not to wish her female competitors to proliferate indefinitely. As more women hold coveted jobs at the workplace, the more they must – like men – scrabble over one another's backs. There's not much room at the pyramid's top.

A recent media trend has been that of media hyenas doing what they do best: creating television programmes about themselves, their values and, of course, starring in them. Such a vision reached BBC 2 in the form of *Last Word*, chaired by Germaine Greer and including an all-female panel comprised of such representative figures as TV mogul Janet Street-Porter; Beatrix Campbell, a writer with a decidedly feminist orientation; Suzanne Moore, columnist for the *Guardian*, well-known for her strong 'opinions' about men; Caitlin Moran, *enfant terrible* and music journalist; and Ann Leslie, Foreign Correspondent for the *Daily Mail*. In the programme, which addressed the woman's role in the workplace, each contributor was asked about the most 'horrible' job they had had to do. Predictably, they cited non-media jobs which are quite representative of most women. It was Ann Leslie who seemed the only one sensitive enough to spot the glaringly obvious:

> When we did this opening round of horrible jobs, I felt actually quite embarrassed because here we are, spoilt darlings of the chattering classes, saying 'oh it was terrible to be doing this, it was terrible to be doing that'. Most people *are* doing that kind of job and I don't think it helps for them to have their self-respect built up and everything by having spoilt darlings like us saying 'oh it was a frightful job'.

The discussion then moved on to the more specific issue of 'The Glass Ceiling', a subject waiting to be given their 'grass roots' perspective:

Street-Porter: Why is it that women don't get promoted at work? . . . Women at the moment, *incredibly*, lack confidence. I interview *lots* of women for jobs and it's as if they're always the cleverest people you interview, but somehow they're not *going* for it.

Campbell: Why don't employers *learn* something from this – which is that the difference between men and women is what's called 'The Bullshit Factor'. So you've got, say, in our profession – which is journalism – a bloke saying 'I've got a cracking story,' and a woman saying 'Well there's a quite interesting story . . . but there's buts and there's buts.' Employers get CVs, they read them, they look at the qualifications – what's the *matter* with them? Why can't they *see* that a woman who's full of scepticism, qualification, is a woman who's *thinking*, rather than a woman who's simply self-doubting and self-defacing.

Disregarding the issue of 'thinking' women, Janet Street-Porter immediately went on to complain about how lonely she is in her executive position because she has no women to talk to. Perhaps, next time she is interviewing, Ms Street-Porter may wish to consider more carefully the possibility of employing women instead of 'bullshitters'.

Surprisingly, many women claim privately that 'power women' are much more likely to, and are much better at, treating their female subordinates like shit. They know just the right buttons to press in order to cause optimum humiliation and the effective decimation of another woman's self-esteem. Men are simply too insensitive to be able to achieve this effectively, and besides, they can always be manipulated into shape if they become difficult.

Media women, however, may not be as 'womanly' as they like to think. According to Dr Malcolm Carruthers, director of a clinic involved in hormone replacement, 'Women who have a competitive, male orientated, achieving life can have up to three times the amount of testosterone of a domiciled, nurturing female. Women who live like men have more testosterone.' Poetic justice, for male chauvinist pigs, was served upon professional feminist Germaine Greer who, upon receiving hormone replacement therapy which included testosterone, was reported to have 'gone wild, [saying] now she knew what it felt like to be a rapist'. One wonders what *The Female Eunuch* would have been like, had she started taking the tablets a quarter of a century earlier.

The boyfriends and husbands of such media women are often 'nice guys', possessing qualities such as reliability, predictability, devotion: important qualities for her male partner to have if she wants to survive and maintain some order in the perilous world in which she works. Retaining control and managing events are important aspects of forming a solid base to operate from. Such a strategy is eminently sensible and has been traditionally employed by professional men. The main flaw appears when such girls recommend these forms of relationships to others. The fact that *they* can co-exist and be sexually aroused by these rather safe male specimens is no reason to assume that women in general can 'choose' to feel such stirrings for these minority males. Media women find it somewhat difficult to comprehend the fact that they and their relationships have little or no relevance to women in general. This behaviour also manifests itself in the workplace where many of these women further reinforce their erroneous views about 'real life' by cocooning themselves with safe male specimens in the form of gay men: small wonder that single media women find themselves lamenting the few opportunities open to them for sexual encounters.

There is, however, an exception to this generality. One would expect that, of all the women likely to adhere strictly to careful choices in male partners, those who run feminist publishing houses would be the ones. Ironically, one of the 'top cats' in just such an organisation is herself apparently not particularly averse to a bit of 'otherness' when it comes to *her* choice of partner, being wed to a man known to drink beer, watch football, and sleep around. This small discrepancy is unlikely to appear when she publishes her own autobiography.

Like so many of the examples proffered by influential media women, the typical Insignificant Other Partner is often suitably attired in regulation non-threatening recovering male uniform: horn-rimmed glasses, chinos, boat shoes. Both he and his politically correct erections are held up as an example to us all. He views her public affirmation that 'he's not into any of that ridiculous macho behaviour' as a compliment. While he may not engage in recreational weeping, he is hardly likely to initiate foreplay with uncaring expressions like 'shut up bitch and open your mouth.' In fact, the exact form of his first manly sexual overture toward her would be more likely to take the form of: 'I love and respect your mind and I'd very much like to have a meaningful relationship with you . . . if that's all right. Shall we talk about it?'

Given the undue influence of the type of women described above, one would have expected a respectable male backlash *à la* Norman Mailer. However, what transpired was rather more of a whimper, or a polite complaint. Several reasonable male authors attempted to challenge the modern picture of man as an insensitive, uncommunicative brute, bent on the oppression of women. Although it was awfully decent of them to attempt to paint a somewhat rosier picture of masculinity, they would have been better advised to simply defend and justify as opposed to deny. Predictably they were unfairly attacked by media feminists and, worse still, by so-called new men. One such author, David Thomas, concluded: 'I have come to understand that nothing on earth is more pathetic than the sight of a man abasing himself before the shrine of politically correct feminism.' The extraordinary thing is the unfair reaction to an eminently sensible reassessment of the sexual agenda.

The basic question as to whether it is possible for grown men in general, or an individual man in particular, to adapt his fundamental behaviours to suit the times is dismissed, for it is still expected that they should do so – or to at least make the effort to change. This leads to the issue of men becoming 'more willing to communicate within relationships'. The assumption is that this practice is purely a matter of 'choice' – an option on the part of the recalcitrant man concerned. Putting emotions into spoken words is considered perfectly natural behaviour for men. With a little re-education, men can cultivate the emotional and verbal skills that have been lying in wait. Such optimism is reinforced by a recent spate of books, programmes and even men's groups. Radio 4 fell prey to the *Zeitgeist* when they formularised the mythology of male changing-room conversations and turned it into a programme entitled *The Locker Room*, hosted by that most representative of heterosexual British males, Mr Tom Robinson, who has still to really make up his mind what he is 'Glad To Be'. *The Locker Room* is portrayed as a vehicle through which men from all walks of life share their feelings on a wide variety of typically manly pursuits, from brands of make-up to impotence, thus providing thinking women with strange ideas about men and what they can expect from them.

What underlies this movement is the belief that men actually talk to each other. However, Garrison Keillor reveals the truth in *The Book of Guys*: 'Guys don't talk to each other. We paw up dirt, bang antlers, sometimes we graze side-by-side, but we seldom talk . . . The biggest myth of all is that men can open up to each other and share their secrets.'

The suicide rate for younger men has doubled in the last ten years and continues to rise unabated. Year after year, the Samaritans in their annual report cite the male inability to articulate emotions as a central factor in explaining why men opt for an early demise as a preferred method of dealing with emotional pain as opposed to simply talking it over. 'The traditional British stiff upper lip shows no sign of trembling, and the reluctance of men to talk about their feelings can often lead to bottling up their emotions which in turn can lead to fatal acts.' Incidentally, female suicides have fallen by 48 per cent during the same period. Nevertheless, it is still assumed that men are, to a large extent, simply being intransigent when it comes to expressing their emotions.

Would it not seem obvious that if it were possible for men to be emotionally articulate, they would certainly choose to be so? This characteristic is reflected in their physiological responses when having to talk about relationships. Studies have found that such verbal expression significantly accelerates a man's heart-rate, much more than it does in a woman. One study concluded that the higher the man's heart-rate the greater the likelihood the marriage would unravel. Even the process of such unravelling – rows – is more physiologically stressful for men; their hearts beat faster, the contractions are sharper and their respiration is faster. A typical fight or flight reaction.

It appears that men are caught in a Catch 22 situation, for despite increasing demands for them to express their emotions and communicate to women, many men find their emotional outpourings greeted with a less than enthusiastic response. Women are terribly ambivalent about the kind of emotions they want to hear expressed. They are not ready to accept men's fears, anger or their sadness, preferring men to be the protectors and providers, roles they will not fulfil, women fear, if they become soft. The greatest act of public duplicity has been committed by RELATE. This organisation prides itself on encouraging men to 'open up' and express their fears and insecurities, to show their vulnerable side and communicate their need for support when necessary. It is therefore most disillusioning to find that, tucked away in their *Guide to Sex in Loving Relationships*, they reveal the extraordinary dishonesty of their editorial line on how men should behave within relationships: 'Although some women welcomed the increase in communication, it was only up to a point. . . . But not when the feelings were negative, or when the men exposed fears and insecurities and appeared weak and in need of support.' Some women were saying of such men that 'they didn't find them sexually attractive, or couldn't respect them. These women thought they wanted an equal relationship, but were unable to cope with it.' A rather extraordinary paradox for the major relationship organisation to have engineered, telling men to open up and express their vulnerable side, but hiding from them their own professional belief that if they went ahead and followed the RELATE line, women would consequently find them sexually unattractive and would be unable to respect them.

The former feminist Marina Warner was invited to deliver the 1994 Reith Lectures. In her second lecture, 'Boys Will Be Boys: The Making of the Male', Warner concludes by referring to Mary Shelley's definition of power in her apocalyptic novel *The Last Man*: 'This I thought is Power! Not to be strong of limb, hard of heart, ferocious and daring; but kind, compassionate and soft.' Warner comments that it is 'a measure of the depths of our present failure of nerve that these words sound ridiculous, embarrassing, inappropriate.' Even beneath the hardest feminist lies a longing for a James Stewart figure in her life; a man who, in addition to being kind and attentive, is actually strong, reliable, consistent, solvent and protective: rather a tall order for non-celluloid males.

Communication, more than any other concept, is considered the most valued and recommended aspect of pursuing improved relationships. By the term 'communication', one is referring to the use of language to convey feeling and emotion. While there has been a recent acknowledgement that men and women use and interpret language differently and that this is a source of much misunderstanding, it is important to realise that, in these emotionally verbose times, language can itself be no more than a most crude approximation of emotion. We place too much confidence in the ability to translate emotion into words. Like Chinese Whispers, the route from heart to mouth is fraught with countless opportunities for inaccuracy. Moreover, unless it is necessary to articulate our feelings, it may be preferable to rely upon more natural forms of communication which have been ignored because they are more idiosyncratic, intuitive and less defined. Simply more grunting perhaps?

For example, your author recently discovered a most effective, intuitive form of communication which can remedy relationship disagreements fairly quickly. My former girlfriend persisted in locating my Achilles tendon and prodding it in order to undermine me when she felt the need. This phenomenon is referred to on assertiveness courses as 'the broken record' technique. Being a psychologist, I went through the various prescribed civilised verbal approaches to dissuade her from resorting to such emotionally underhanded ways of relating to me. I also feigned ennui so as not to provide her with 'positive reinforcement for counterproductive behaviours within our relationship.' All of these to no avail. One evening, however, I inadvertently stumbled across the solution. After listening to the broken record again, I went through the usual motions of communicating to her how I felt about her assertions. Predictably this had little effect. It was only ten minutes later when I stared into the refrigerator that I saw the answer to our communication problems staring straight back at me. It was an iceberg lettuce. What Delia doesn't tell you is that an iceberg lettuce is not just for eating. While it didn't provide on-the-spot counselling, it was the perfect vehicle for expressing my emotions – so I threw it at my girlfriend's much prized and rather tidy spice rack. After seeing a new mixed-spice and broken glass recipe appearing before my eyes on the kitchen floor, I could feel my blood pressure stabilising rapidly. This served to further my interest in this new 'smashing therapy'; I could even see an academic paper in it for me somewhere. So I then turned my attention to other ingredients and of course, wishing to return the iceberg lettuce to its right and proper place, as well as having further emotions to communicate, hurled it back into the fridge at 150 miles an hour. My blood pressure returned to normal. Moreover, the broken record spontaneously repaired itself among the spicy shards. Being a repressed male can be an exciting gastronomic experience, unless you're an iceberg lettuce.

While other repressed males are busy contending with their

emotional barriers, women are busy bumping their heads on The Glass Ceiling. It is 'common knowledge' that women do not rule the world and do not get paid as much for not ruling the world, because they are not as assertive as men and even if they were, male values would prevail anyway, blocking their path. There is also the issue of children. So, the assumption is that if the Equal Opportunities Commission ever becomes successful enough to disband, women will have ascended to the same levels that had previously been occupied almost exclusively by men. This will never happen, not because men will not allow it, but because women just don't have what it takes. They do have the abilities necessary to rule the world and, indeed, would probably do a much better job of it. What they lack is the obsession with achieving power at all costs that afflicts men. This obsession is not a product of conditioning, rather, a biological imperative. Ironically it is women who have the natural capacity to listen, read people's needs and tell them what they want to hear – in the commercial world, this translates into superior consumer empathy followed by supplying the demand, exploiting and oppressing – the ideal capitalists.

Ironically, while there has been much lamentation concerning women's relative position on the ladder pointing toward a 'successful' life, few have bothered to question whether there is more than one ladder. Men on the whole have a much narrower conception of 'success' which is inextricably linked to their careers and can be undertaken in a linear fashion, upwards. Men are the ones who kill themselves over the loss of a job or lack of promotion: they are the gender which sacrifices its health, close friendships and family life for the sake of achieving 'success'. They are the sex which, on the scabrous road to success, dies prematurely at roughly twice the rate that women do from the twelve principal causes of death. It's a good life – Come On Down!

Success for women generally is more diffuse, possessing far greater breadth. A well-rounded life with a strong emphasis upon 'quality' relationships, family, and the sonorous, if not instantaneous, gratification of producing, nurturing and rearing children. They rarely kill themselves over trivial matters such as work-related issues and, unlike their male counterparts, they are protected from the ravages of work by an awesome array of biological mechanisms. In fact, several studies have found that women's health actually *improves* when they enter the workplace. For example, while women may fail to appreciate the aesthetic qualities of the harmless fat which lies on their hips and thighs, men process dietary fats differently and more dangerously. Instead of finding their way to a man's hips and thighs, they migrate' to his arteries, which, like his character, are far less flexible: women's arteries are more pliable in order to accommodate a possible foetus: blood for two. Furthermore, men and their arteries are predisposed to react aggressively and rapidly to challenge and stress, and such endearing traits exact a high cost. The mortality rate for premature heart disease among men is four times that of women.

There is an interesting side to this. Researchers have for some time noticed a correlation between personality types which are domineering, aggressive, repressed, hostile – and premature death from heart disease. Such a personality is referred to as Type A. Interestingly, almost all the research on this phenomenon has been carried out on men. One area of research takes place in a laboratory setting and involves irritating men and then measuring the physiological effects. When the author asked one of the research scientists why they didn't include women in their studies, he was told that it was 'far too time consuming and expensive to irritate women in a laboratory at short notice.' It was easy to raise the blood pressure of a man: one simply gives him a task to carry out on a computer programme –

and then 'challenges' him by sabotaging the programme in mid-course. Predictably, men would huff and puff, becoming frustrated as a result of the software obstruction, and their blood pressure would rise. To produce an equivalent response in a woman would have involved a more people-orientated design – and one can only fit so many irritating people into a single laboratory. It would take a theatre director of some note to carry it off convincingly.

In an attempt to discredit much 'inconvenient' male behaviour, the term 'the male ego' has become a reflexive panacea. Such a euphemism implies that the ego in question is the result of a conscious choice to posture, brag and be generally intransigent and self-centred. In other words, the male ego is an unnecessary hindrance which has been allowed to continue unchecked for too long. Consequently, great efforts should be put into pushing the male ego out of business. However, the above characteristics are the very *essence* of being male, and attempts at eliminating them would ultimately benefit no-one. It also has to be said that if psychology placed similar pressures to change upon, for example, blacks or homosexuals, the cacophony of protesting voices would be deafening.

A further area for misunderstanding, but one which is happily exploited by psychology, is the perceived disparity in self-esteem, confidence and assertiveness between men and women. These characteristics are seen as distinct entities of which men possess more than women. Great effort has been put into 'empowering' women through, for example, assertiveness training, in an attempt to raise their self-esteem and confidence to the levels men are assumed to have. Not only is this considered important in terms of work opportunities, but it is also important in love. While, at one time, women were not expected to have much sexual self-confidence and assertiveness, being on the receiving end of men's gratification, they are now being encouraged to

objectify members of the opposite sex. However, these characteristics manifest themselves in different ways in men and
women. There are also differences in the types of achievement
that can influence their respective self-esteem. While males
respond more to corporeal forms of achievement, women are
more appreciative of 'affiliate achievement' involving the quality
of their relationships.

Many women feel that, in a number of ways, they have
failed. But they have only failed to be men. Unfortunately, at
the moment, the strongest influences on women's definition of
success are the 'successful' women foisted upon them by the
media which has different motives for presenting the images
they do. This has again left some women feeling unsuccessful
in attaining the desired levels of these qualities.

What we commonly perceive as self-esteem, confidence and
assertiveness are strongly linked to aggression, a quality lavished
upon men. For those who haven't noticed, men are also far more
single-minded, selfish and insensitive to others, characteristics
which, combined with the propulsive effects of testosterone,
are suited to 'achieving' in the more conventional sense of the
word. Such achievements may pass as the successful result of
'high' self-esteem. Society has more recently been presented
with 'successful' female role-models in the form of television
and film actresses, who appear to possess significant levels of
high self-esteem (and very insignificant levels of body fat), which
carries the connotation that 'they got to the top because they
liked themselves.' However, it could just as easily be said that
they 'got to the top' precisely because they *didn't* like themselves
and needed the intense, albeit not always reliable, adulation,
approval and reassurance which fame brings with it, just in
order to 'feel good about themselves'. Those unfamiliar with *the*
industry may be labouring under the misapprehension that it is
a rather sexy world, staffed by sensuous, self-confident women

whose opportunities for 'satisfying' relationships are greater, whose passions run deeper, whose orgasms are more abundant and intense. However, long hours on the set and stolen moments sticking one's fingers down one's throat, don't actually leave a girl with much time and energy for 'quality time' in which to indulge in such pursuits. There is also precious little time for being caring, sharing and supportive.

Nurturing and caring seem simple enough qualities but they are not distributed equally between the sexes. Nevertheless it is commonly believed that with the right social conditions, men can develop these skills and apply them both to relationships and to parenting. Media images of the 'New Father' give the impression that men in general can simply change in order to play an equal part in the task of child-rearing. Encouraging the sexes to be more alike within relationships has been extended to the outcome of their relationships: parenthood. In the trend toward a more neutral form of parenting, mothers and fathers have been advised not to emphasise the stereotypical, traditional 'man and woman' role-modelling. This approach, it is hoped, will provide children with a less rigid outlook, widening the horizons of boys and girls as they later consider careers, lifestyles and relationships, as well as liberalising their behaviour. As a redefinition of fatherhood has been underway, even Dr Spock has bowed to political pressure by carefully revising his advice on the subject. In the earlier version of *Baby and Child Care*, he suggested that fathers occasionally change the nappies, and cautioned mothers about 'trying to force the participation of fathers who get gooseflesh at the very idea of helping to take care of a baby.' On the other hand, a later edition suggested that: 'The father – any father – should be sharing with the mother the day-to-day care of their child from birth onward . . . This is the natural way for the father to start the relationship, just as it is for the mother.' However, both research and common sense show that men parent differently from women – and that these differences are enormously important. Some of the uniquely male contributions that are essential for raising children are being ignored or even discouraged in the move toward a more shared child-rearing. The trend toward the 'New Father' leaves a family with a mother and an assistant mother; this can be highly detrimental to both the children and the parents' own relationship. As parents, men and women are suited to different roles at different times; the parenting of young infants is not a natural activity for males. Researchers have remarked at the general differences between the way mothers and fathers respond to their offspring. Fathers are more likely to treat infants as pets, 'things' rather than individuals with whom one can interact. But as time passes, the strengths that fathers may bring to child-rearing become more important. A father is particularly skilled at producing socially *viable* children, preparing them for life's rough and tumble, familiarising them with the idea of rules and the consequences of disregarding them. A mother's love is perceived by the child as 'unconditional', the father's love is more qualified and related to the child's performance. While mothers worry about the infant's survival, fathers are concerned with its future success. Discipline consists of a combination of mother and father: justice tempered by mercy. Fathers are more likely to discipline by 'rules', and children acquire an awareness of their emotional side from their mothers. The father teaches them how to live in society. Fathers should thus be more than merely assistant mothers.

These observations are generalisations, 'norms'. They are not intended as a cultural imperative, but rather a more realistic and representative framework from which to view fatherhood. Animal species in which the male shares the parental duties are characterised by physical and other similarities between the two sexes. This seems to be the case in humans as well – the more 'feminine' the man, the greater his involvement is likely to be in baby care. Despite this, it is these men who are put forward as an example to be 'followed' by other men; it's all about 'choosing' to be more nurturing and caring. Interestingly, in terms of the proportion of men who change nappies and help with the housework, very little has changed in the last thirty years.

Placing political wishes aside, parents should also be aware that, as men and women, they are inculcating their children with ideas about the characteristics they will expect to find in men and women in general. In their book *The Father–Daughter Dance*, psychologists Barbara Goulter and Joan Minninger examine the influence of fathers. They reinforce the idea that a girl's father becomes a reference point for all other males, shaping her expectations of their behaviour toward her. By providing children with a more androgynous frame of reference, are parents really preparing their children for the world as it truly is?

A failure to acknowledge the profound differences between men and women as parents can also rebound upon the marriage itself. The past couple of years has seen a growing concern about the effects that absent fathers have upon children. More children are being reared in fatherless homes than ever before. This issue has a slightly different emphasis than the furore over single motherhood. The reasons for such a high level of absent fathers are also open to new interpretation. Despite women's demands for the greater involvement of men with their children, many women are somewhat ambivalent in their interpretation of such involvement. Many women have been found to jealously guard their domestic power, thus acting as gatekeepers in the home. Time and time again, men report that the message conveyed to them is, 'we'd very much like you to be involved – but you'll be an inadequate mother.' While various explanations have been offered to help explain the causes of the high divorce rate, researchers have returned to a rather obvious explanation which has been overlooked in favour of more exciting alternatives: the arrival of the first child. Contrary to an increased sense of togetherness, the vast majority of relationships undergo a notable degree of crisis upon the first birth. Becoming parents affects each sex differently. Although it may appear a cliché, a father is more inclined to resent what he perceives as the reallocation of love and affection, these being seen as measurable 'resources'. Given the male proclivity to viewing things within a competitive, hierarchical framework, this is not surprising. Therefore, it is neither 'childish' nor unduly 'selfish' for fathers to respond in this way. Conversely, new mothers consider their child as a development of their sexual relationship, not an alternative to it. Women are endowed with the artful ability to accommodate a broader range of relationships without rejecting or weakening any of them – love for their child is not 'at the expense of' anyone else. This contrast in predispositions is not the product of conditioning, ignorance or choice. Coupled with the fact that many women still consider a man's earning power as *the* primary factor determining his suitability as a prospective mate and father, many fathers find these competing demands too much to contend with. Research has shown that fatherhood is, by its very evolutionary nature, more frail than motherhood and therefore is in need of encouragement by the mother and by society. Fathers require substantial social and emotional reinforcement in order to remain within the family unit and perform their vital role in bringing up children.

Given the ever-changing economic conditions, together with the woman's desire to seek self-fulfilment through her career, the question of who cares and nurtures best is becoming more of an issue. There are new expectations and it is now felt that, when it comes to child-rearing, things are unequal and unfair. It is often pointed out that, as women are always going to be left 'holding the baby', they will always be at a disadvantage. Mothers, however, are natural carers and nurturers, fathers are not. That it is the mothers who are better at reading their baby's needs, who have a superior ability to hear and identify their own baby crying, and a greater sensitivity to touch, sound and smell, is not a coincidence. For example, the crying of a baby produces the immediate secretion of a hormone which causes a mother's nipples to become erect in preparation for breastfeeding.

The facility for superior nurturing and caring begins even before the mother herself is born and seems to be related directly to the exposure to female, as opposed to male, hormones in the womb. Women exposed to large amounts of male hormone whilst in the womb (either because their mothers were receiving male hormones for medical reasons, or because as a foetus they had an abnormality resulting in the production of male hormone) exhibit little, if any, maternal inclinations. Conversely, foetuses which have an extra female chromosome and no exposure whatsoever to male hormones, display heightened maternal inclinations. Moreover, by the time a child is born, there has been a nine-month period of attachment and a relationship has already formed. Little wonder that so many surrogate mothers cannot bear to keep their promise. Therefore, how can one ever expect there to be 'equality' in the capacity to care and nurture. Convenient or not, this is not a question of equality, rather, a matter of differences in aptitude which are undeniable.

Women are also left holding a rather bigger baby, for they almost always take on the role of caretaker within their relationship. It is often said that women put more energy into a relationship: they listen more, worry more and initiate difficult discussions about relationship matters. Given the escalating suicide rate amongst men, more would probably end their lives if women were not there to listen and help unburden them. For example, Vietnam war veterans suffering from post-traumatic stress syndrome were found to open up to women more easily when it came to discussing the painful emotional legacy of their experiences of the war. Sadly, even a most well-respected and prominent female psychotherapist has referred to this female *strength* in the most derogatory terms when she described it as 'the refuse system for cleaning up the emotions', whilst an academic feminist paper, in its title, described it as *Interactional Shit-Work*. Worse than washing a man's socks.

On a wider note, as previously mentioned, it is also women who are the caretakers of family relationships, trying to ensure that their family remains cohesive. This proclivity too is not the product of conditioning; it is merely an extension of the nurturing and caring characteristics inherent in their make-up. What this means in practical terms is that the relationship between the sexes is based upon complementary strengths. Women are far stronger in verbal and emotional areas and so the burden of maintaining relationships and families will naturally fall upon their shoulders. Men should *not* be expected to have an equal share in this burden. They don't have what it takes. Suggestions that men can change substantially in this direction are counterproductive and have left many a woman feeling disappointed, unsuccessful, inadequate, his short-comings seen merely as a reflection of her worth. Yet another example of how raising expectations can actually lower self-esteem.

The redefinition of the roles of men and women is a phenomenon not confined to the stripped-pine dinner tables of Islington. Japan is now experiencing a new period of 'adjustment' between husbands and wives which serves as a salutary lesson to us all. Japanese women are becoming increasingly dissatisfied with the traditional behaviour of their men, known for their paucity of chat and dirth of geisha, and, contrary to the approach adopted by their Western counterparts of trying to change their men, have wisely accepted the futility of such an exercise.

For they understand that if you want someone to be caring, sharing, romantic, attentive and supportive, you engage the most suitably qualified person for the job: a woman. 'Takarazuka' is an all-female musical theatre company where the male roles are all played by women. What is most interesting is that these 'women-men' are treated like pop stars, are regularly mobbed by their women admirers, receive fan mail and even offers of marriage. There are also night clubs hosted by 'women-men', where women can live out their fantasies of being properly 'treated like a lady'. On the male front, Japan's Education Minister has launched special classes to teach businessmen how to talk to their wives and spend more time taking part in family life. More than half of all 13 and 14 year olds never talk to their fathers.

A most disturbing outcome of various notions associated with contemporary psychology is the blatant attempt at socially engineering the next generation. Sadly, the Family Planning Association, bastion of sensible sex education and contraception, has associated itself with *How Sex Works* – the 'authoritative and factual guide to every aspect of growing up, starting relation-ships and becoming sexually mature' – intended for all schools and teenagers. While the technical information is more than adequate, the 'real' emotional information is sadly wanting and, in some cases, wrong. The authors categorically fail to recognise gender differences in relationships and sexuality for young people. Neither in the table of contents nor in the index is there any acknowledgement whatsoever of these differences. This is rather shocking when one stands back and considers that sex and romance is all about 'otherness' – two different sexes coming together. Just a little footnote would have been nice. This is not simply an oversight, but is quite intentional, for the authors make clear their antipathy toward generalisations and stereotypes and hope to overturn gender differences by stressing to young people that such differences do not and should not exist: 'Stereotypes are inaccurate and unfair. They encourage you to think of someone as a type because of their gender ... rather than as an individual. ... Old rules about sexual relationships need not apply today ... it is better to view people as individuals than to prejudge them on the basis of sex.' Is providing young people with realistic expectations of the sexuality and temperament of the opposite sex 'inaccurate and unfair'? Curiously, after a long diatribe attacking racial stereotyping, they provide young people with the following, entitled 'Enriching Experience': 'If you live in a multi-cultural area, you will probably mix with people whose backgrounds are very different from your own.' So, on the one hand, they detest forming a stereotype based upon 'colour or appearance, rather than as an individual', whilst strangely, they inform you that, if you see a person who looks ethnically different, you should immediately assume that they *are* very different from you.

A recognition of otherness is conspicuous by its absence in most 'helping' organisations. When the young are exposed to the above ideas and later find themselves in need of the services of RELATE, they are immediately advised to go on a witchhunt to identify and eliminate any generalisations about the sexes which may have contributed to the downfall of their relationships. In an attempt to drum out generalisations from the human condition, *The RELATE Guide to Starting Again* invites the reader to engage in exercises to achieve this very aim. The exercise entitled 'Men and Women' carries the instructions: 'Without pausing to think, fill in these sections with as many generalisations as come into your mind about what men and women think, want and how they usually behave.' The pursuit of generalisations does not relent, culminating finally in an attempt to identify those who '*formed* your ideas' about the sexes, through partaking in a '*Task*' entitled 'Who Started It?'. One is instructed to 'Look back at your lists' of the generalisations identified in the previous exercises and 'Put the initials of the person who told you how men and women are' after each generalisation. In the three main RELATE books, there is little or no mention of gender differences, indicating a concerted effort to ignore them. The benefits to the reader of ignoring these differences are spelled out: 'You are free to choose someone who behaves differently from your earlier expectations, so that a more rewarding relationship is possible.' This is indicative of the consumer orientation of 'managing' emotions, sex and relationships, regularly conveyed by the language in which they are discussed: 'free' . . . 'choose' . . . 'rewarding'. To focus upon such detail may seem pedantic; however, it is the ideology which underlies these misguided or politically motivated passages within the publications of such major institutions that is most concerning.

Those involved in educational policy are also guilty of ignoring fundamental differences in intellect between boys and girls. Their oversight has, unfortunately for the children involved in such an equal opportunity approach to education, now come home to roost. It has for some time been fashionable to believe that boys and girls should have a chance to do equally well in all academic subjects. Any disparity in performance was explained away as the result of, for example, boys being encouraged to do well at maths and science. To question this explanation and suggest that there may be profound biological differences in aptitude was to invite accusations ranging from the sexual-political – 'sexism' – to the party-political – 'right wing traditionalist'. The Government has finally acknowledged a serious gulf in performance in English between boys and girls. Girls are almost twice as likely to get a GCSE grade A as boys, and the gap is widening. However, a gap in verbal abilities has always existed. During early adolescence, girls begin to out-perform boys on tests of verbal ability, and this female superiority persists into adulthood. Now, ironically, the Government is allowing mixed comprehensive schools to reintroduce single-sex classes for English lessons in an attempt to improve the poor performance of boys. They will be placed in smaller classes than girls, receive extra tuition in the specific writing skills they lack and, in an attempt to encourage them to read fiction, they will be presented with more 'masculine' texts. The Education Secretary said: 'It's the sort of imaginative way of trying to drive up standards.' Terms such as 'imaginative' neither address the roots of the problem nor apologise for the previous ignoring of fundamental differences in aptitude between Janet and John. The differential between boys and girls is also found in private education. In 1994, for example, out of 623 fee-paying schools, the top six, according to GCSE results, were all-girls schools.

Research from all over the world has consistently found a male superiority in visual-spatial ability, e.g. analysing and mentally manipulating three-dimensional objects, which begins to show up around the age of eight and persists into old age. This has not escaped the notice of Mary Dejevsky of the *Independent*, who wrote an article about the male bias contained within the design of computer software, entitled 'Why *Windows* is a feminist issue.' While she was being retrained at the *Independent* to use a new computer, she recounted: 'I realised with a flash of recognition what was wrong: this was a *man*'s computer world . . . the aptitudes required to make these systems easy and enjoyable are all those associated with maleness.' Males also display an advantage in higher mathematics, such as algebra. At the very top of the ability scale, the gap between boys and girls is quite profound and certainly isn't due to cultural factors, conditioning or any other social phenomenon. Moreover, it isn't sheer coincidence that girls who have received abnormal doses of testosterone in the womb appear to do better than average on tests of higher mathematical ability, and boys with an abnormality that makes their cells insensitive to testosterone's effects have intellectual profiles identical to girls': their verbal IQ is higher than in normal males, and their 'performance' IQ (correlated with mechanical ability), is inferior to that of normal males. Those tempted to facilitate their entry to Oxbridge through this form of hormonal self-improvement should, however, be aware that acquiring a First in maths may also involve acquiring a beard, moustache and a bad attitude. It is also interesting to observe that female athletes who are disqualified for taking hormones are invariably discovered to be taking *male*, not female hormones in order to increase their strength and *aggression*: their 'winning behaviour'. Ben Johnson was not taking oestrogen.

The above examples are a reflection of the fact that the male and female brains are very different and their respective hormones only make matters worse – a fact not subject to over-emphasis by the psychology presented to most people. In women, for instance, abilities such as language appear to be more evenly divided between the left and right halves of the brain; in men they are much more confined to the left half. After strokes or injuries to the left half of the brain, women are three times less likely than men to suffer language problems. Such differences are not restricted to intellectual abilities alone, for they permeate every area of the human condition including the ability to express emotions, assertiveness and aggression, nurturing and caring and sexual behaviour.

Final proof of the inevitability of gender differences comes in the form of the failed attempts to do away with The Jewish Mother. The Israeli kibbutz is more than a summer haven for British university students seeking to experience commune life through picking fruit. One of the main aims of the kibbutz was to create an entirely self-contained community in which males and females adopt virtually interchangeable roles. The community as a whole is responsible for child-rearing and household duties such as cooking and washing: men and women doing their equal share of the work. The expectation was that after several 'genderless' generations, sexual differences would disappear and sexist stereotyping would simply not exist. Unfortunately, this utopian vision was not realised. Even after the fourth generation, kibbutz children are still conforming to their traditional stereotypes and the women are returning to their maternal roles. Despite ideology, socialisation, the economic interests of the community and even against the ideological wishes of their men, little has changed and The Jewish Mother lives on to cook another chicken soup. However, being both an 'ologist' and the son of such a mother and grandmother before her, not to mention having a daughter who failed to play war games with me, I did not find it necessary to consult the scientific literature to arrive at these rather foregone conclusions.

Despite the volumes of new literature which attempt to provide 'fresh, new ideas' about 'where male and female relationships are going', the fact remains that there are no 'fresh, new ideas': nothing has changed except our expectations. Attempts to 'sophisticate' the relationship between the sexes may make interesting reading, but add nothing and, in many respects, detract from the truth which is, and always has been, terribly simple. Rudimentary explanations for our respective behaviours are often dismissed as mere trivial popular socio-biology for the masses, a bit of light entertainment before the real 'issues' are considered. This has had very unfortunate consequences. Such intellectual accounts attempt to provide substance to a subject which would otherwise make rather dull, uninspiring and very short reading. There are, in fact, a number of superb books about 'socio-biology' which seem to be preaching to the converted. Much of the reason for this state of affairs lies in the fact that neither science nor scientists are known for their entertainment value and they are notoriously reluctant to rub in the political and social implications of their observations. Moreover, unlike the Arts and humanities, science has only turned its attention to the human condition in the last hundred years. Hormones were first identified in 1902 and university degree courses addressing the neurophysiological basis of behaviour are a recent development. It would therefore seem natural to prefer to entrust the examination of our human relationships to those who we perceive as being more 'human' and caring: authors, humanistic psychologists and earnest discussions on late-night Arts programmes; a cuddly story about our nature which allows us to sleep more easily at night.

It is tempting to resolve the gulf between the sexes by an all too obvious and pragmatic approach, i.e. reducing the amount of testosterone in men. This would seem a logical step. Neutered tom cats, for instance, live on average two years longer than their 'intact' brothers. Part of the reason is that they are more conciliatory – 'New Cats' – and less likely to die in fights. However, even if one considers only the cats that die of natural causes, the neutered toms still live longer. Spaying females doesn't affect their life-spans. Those unconvinced by such basic animal examples may be interested in the effects of castration upon men. Until 1950, psychiatric hospitals in the United States would sometimes castrate their male patients, usually with the intent of rendering them more docile. One research team studied 297 men who had been castrated at an institution for the mentally retarded in Kansas. These 'New Men' outlived an 'intact' group of male patients by nearly 14 years. Even more surprising, they also outlived a comparable group of female patients. Of course, there are disadvantages to such an abrupt change of character.

The politically expedient belief that we are all born as blank canvases upon which society paints its sexist impasto is naive in the extreme. The fact that we have a more highly developed cerebrum than other animals does not change the fact that males and females of *all* species are profoundly different from birth. Being more intelligent as a species may provide men and women with greater insight into their respective differences, but doesn't for a moment make them any more alike. Therefore, should it not in fact be those who cling to the notion of inherent 'sameness' who should substantiate their new-found philosophy: after all, countless millennia of incompatibility can't be wrong. As writer Sabine Reichel observes: 'This archaic and basically primitive relationship between men and women is dark, irrational and turbulent, defined by ambivalence. Sex and its seductive and urgent powers are not about fairness, niceness and equality.' Or, as Rodgers & Hart put it:

> *Believe me Sir*
> *I much prefer*
> *The classic battle of a him and her*
> *I don't like quiet*
> *And I wish I were in love again*

5: Someone to Cling to as the Ship Goes Down . . .

Relationships do have a way of making gender differences shine, or possibly glare. When attempting to engage in such a union with a member of the opposite sex, many of the issues raised in the previous chapter come to the fore. It should be quite apparent by now that, instead of attempting to converge, men and women must come to fully appreciate and understand the profound, irreversible and valid differences between them. This task hasn't been made any easier by contemporary psychological thinking which has continued to promote the idea of a 'compromise' or 'solution' to such an intractable problem. However, these efforts would have been better directed at helping people come to terms with the fact that there *are* no compromises or solutions: a state of détente can only be attained if men and women do what they have always done – agree to disagree. Each gender needs a deeper and uncompromising insight into the workings of the other. Therefore some stereotypes and generalisations, in other words, reference points, could prove immensely useful and reassuring after three decades of 'anything goes'.

Ironically, the greatest understanding of men and women in heterosexual relationships can be gleaned through observing homosexual relationships, in which the sexes are free to express their true natural characteristics unbridled by consideration for the other. As the standing joke among gay men and lesbians goes:

Q. What does a lesbian bring with her on her second date?

A. A removal van.

Q. What does a gay bring with him on his second date?

A. What second date?

In the aptly named London men's gay bar, Brief Encounter, the few women customers who find themselves caught-short, are required to get the key to the Ladies room from the bar. This is not a deliberate policy to discourage women from making this bar their local, but is kept on the grounds that, given the chance, men would occupy the facility in order to consummate their own brief encounter. What a gender!

If one compares the sexual activity of gay men and lesbians, there is a stark contrast which is immediately evident. 'Cottaging' (the practice of anonymous sex in public conveniences) is not a pastime for many lesbians. It is quite apparent that once females (the gatekeepers) are removed from the sexual arena, males can, and will, attempt to fertilise and move on (and on and on). What goes on between men setting up cottage together provides the keenest insight into man's very nature. Such an encounter will involve no emotional or verbal exchanges whatsoever. Once eye-contact is firmly established at the urinals, participants will hastily enter one of the cubicles together. Typically, a shopping bag is placed on the floor: this is not a confirmation of the stereotypical gay's love of shopping, but serves for one of them to stand in whilst the other positions himself on the loo seat, in readiness. Should anyone happen to look under the door, it will appear, to all intents and purposes, that the person on the loo has been to Liberty's, rather than that he is taking liberties.

Another institution frequented exclusively by gay men is the infamous 'pet shop', a 'specialist' section of a more hard-core gay club. Such a venue is not exactly a favourite haunt of animal rights activists or lesbians. For while the name may evoke childhood memories of budgies and hamsters looking hopefully through the bars of their cages for a new home, in this pet shop, small domestic pets are invited to burrow up the bottom of an ecstatic male recipient.

Gay sexuality is honest and can serve as a useful reference point. Straight heterosexuality can never be totally truthful. While the majority of gay men do not lead the above lifestyle, they do have access to a far greater number of sexual partners, and their relationships do not necessarily require the kind of emotional input and conversation seen in heterosexual liaisons.

Sadly, there are those who, in trying to 'protect' gay men from homophobia, deny reality. RELATE, for example, in their *Guide to Sex in Loving Relationships*, suggest that the high productivity seen in the gay world is a symptom of 'emotional or other problems'. They also believe that the hostility and prejudice experienced by gay men has resulted in a sub-culture characterised by 'promiscuity' whereby 'some homosexuals – needing to fit in – have gone along with this, sometimes against their own inclinations.' In point of fact, if gay men are 'promiscuous', it is because, like heterosexual men, they simply love to have lots of sex with lots of partners, but *unlike* heterosexual men, they don't have to contend with, or talk to, women. It is purely a question of opportunity and access, not of 'emotional problems' or the sexual consequences of being an oppressed minority group.

On the academic front, the British Psychological Society has addressed 'Psychological Issues in Gay Male Sexuality' in which research was presented on 'gay men's subjective understandings of anal intercourse' which 'refuted any idea of a simplistic or necessary connection between gay men and anal intercourse'.

The intention of such statements being to convince people that gay men are no more likely to engage in anal intercourse. Again, gay men simply do more of what many heterosexual men would do given half a chance. It would be most interesting to witness a researcher entering a gay bar on behalf of the British Psychological Society, informing the clientele that they all have emotional problems and that there is 'no necessary connection between gay men and anal intercourse'. The point is that, by denying some aspects of reality, one ends up showing a lack of tolerance toward the 'minority group' one is trying 'to protect'. Moreover, in this case, not only are gay men misrepresented, but by virtue of this, so are heterosexual men.

Lesbians are also unbridled by intimate contact with the opposite sex and so they are afforded the luxury of conducting relationships on their own terms, based upon the more 'female' values such as commitment, fulfilling relationships, talking, caring tenderness, plenty of extended foreplay, synchronised menstrual cycles and cosy evenings together reciting passages of de Beauvoir to each other. And, of course, sharing the same cat: the only 'pet' *they* have. Lesbians by and large lead rather unassuming lives compared to their gay male counterparts, which is another of the reasons why it's generally so hard to identify them.

In discussing gender, whether homosexual or heterosexual, D. Symons, in *The Evolution of Human Sexuality*, summarises rather neatly: 'Among men, sex sometimes results in intimacy; in women, intimacy sometimes results in sex.' Men often need sex in order to relax, while women need to relax in order to have sex. Books are still being written, and published, in which every pelvic thrust becomes heavily pregnant with political implications. Lynne Segal, for instance, in her book *Straight Sex* (Virago) suggests that 'dominant social discourses' stress 'the polarity of "active" and "passive", which roped to masculinity and femininity via the existing conception of heterosexuality, must itself be challenged if we are ever to turn around the oppressive cultural hierarchies of gender and sexuality.'!!! When I presented this woman's argument to Fred Bloggs in my gym's changing room, he replied: 'Foking el lady, all I wanna do is stick it in.'

It is interesting to hear the view of a woman with a dual perspective. A female bi-sexual friend of mine is convinced that 'recreational sex is a cul-de-sac for men – a road which leads to very little. Women on the other hand have opened this cul-de-sac, making it into a ring road.' Moreover, it is ironic to hear a woman assess the pros and cons of bedding other women as opposed to men: 'The problem you have with going to bed with a lesbian is that you won't get out for quite a few hours – they don't know the meaning of a quickie. If it wasn't for the fact that somebody's got to feed the cat, you'd be in bed all day.'

Despite talk of there being a 'gay community', gay men and lesbians generally have little to do with one another and don't get on particularly well. This is hardly surprising when one considers that each group has been able to gravitate toward the characteristics of their own sex with little consideration of the opposite sex, which is, to all intents and purposes, out of their frame of reference. A further indication of the healthy lack of inherent compatibility between men and women in general.

The greatest area of incompatibility would appear to be the issue of fidelity, monogamy and sexual appetite which are central to many relationships and their demise. With a strong emphasis on couples achieving some degree of parity within relationships, the prevailing wisdom on conducting better relationships studiously avoids the fact that what is considered sauce for the goose is certainly not suitable for the gander. Much political pressure has been directed at helping society realise that male sexual behaviour need not be a phallocentric mania, but rather an urge that can and should be subject to great deliberation, control, choice and change. Men, we are told, have traditionally been more unfaithful and promiscuous because they have been 'allowed to get away with it', and women have been less so because they and their reproductive capacities have been tightly controlled by their male 'owners'. In addition to this, they have also been 'conditioned' to be more monogamous. It has been the middle classes, the therapy classes, who seem terribly concerned with 'doing the right thing' in a sexual–political sense and have consequently ended up confused. The upper classes display a more unashamed attitude to sex, despite their emotional containment and concern for discretion in so many other matters, generally considering sex a basic animal-world necessity which one simply does: men are beasts, pure and simple.

There have been two main responses to this impasse in fidelity. The first involves the idea that male sexuality can be somehow 'adjusted' to suit modern times. This has, by and large, failed miserably and it may well be that such 'adjustments' have indirectly contributed to the creation of a more hostile and frustrated modern male. The more recent approach invokes an imaginary element of parity when discussing infidelity. This was first seen during the late 1970s, an era when women were encouraged to reach their potential through a flurry of orgasms and the enjoyment of multiple partners: quantity mattered. This was referred to as sexual emancipation and it failed miserably. Women woke up the next morning feeling at fault – less than 'right on' – because they wanted to ask the man lying next to them what his name was and when they would be seeing him again.

We are now informed that 'recent British surveys showed that 40 per cent of females are unfaithful'. Entire books are now published which claim to show just how unfaithful women can be. This is intended to suggest that women and men are much more alike than was previously thought and fits in neatly with the fashionable need to assert that women are 'empowered', women are 'in control' of their own sexuality and now find themselves in a position to 'choose' who and what they want sexually. Who would believe that people tell the truth about their level of fidelity, or their level of income for that matter, in a 'survey'? What sort of person offers to respond to such surveys: representative people? What never seems to accompany such triumphant revelations of female predatory behaviour, is an elucidation of the *context* in which female infidelity occurs and the actual number of illicit liaisons involved. There are marked differences in the nature of infidelity between men and women, which, though clichéd, are nevertheless generally true, and rather telling. Those who stubbornly persist in denying this are in the habit of providing extraordinary examples of rare animal species in which the female fucks the male and then bullies him into doing a bit of hunting and gathering – or an obscure tribe in which the women are polygamous, 'milking' the men as necessary.

While these accounts may be very interesting and entertaining, the reason they are so very interesting and entertaining is precisely because they are highly exceptional and have little to offer in terms of how we should assess our own state of affairs. We now live in a 'measuring' society where all ideas must be quantified in order to appear valid. We have left behind more appropriate research techniques, such as *mass observation*, popular during the 1930s, or *phenomenology*, the study of unanalysed experience. One can refer to animal studies, cross-cultural studies and 'surveys', or one could simply sit back and observe human nature.

Let us leave the 'campus lab' and survey answers of 'sophomores' at mid-western American universities and travel instead to Amsterdam in Spring, where the sexual economy can be seen in action, there to observe what men actually *do* as opposed to what they *say*.

Oudezijds Voorburgwal and Oudezijds Achterburgwal are the two main canals on which prostitutes sell themselves in their 'shop windows'. Being Dutch, it is all terribly civilised. As is the case with restaurant districts such as Paris's Latin Quarter, different nationalities of women can be found on different sections of the canals to make shopping easier and a much more convenient experience. Black Nigerian 'cuisine', for instance, is served on Oude Kerkesplein situated ironically in front of the famous fourteenth-century Old Church; Venezuelan, Colombian and Brazilian dishes are available on the northern part of both canals; Thai can be found along the two narrow lanes that join the two canals, while Holland's own national dishes position themselves brashly in the more grand, imposing windows on the southern end of the canals. An eclectic combination of flavours reside in the various lanes and alleyways which serve as tributaries to the main promenade.

On any given day, hundreds if not thousands of men will embark upon their shopping expeditions within this small district. There are days when the streets are impassable due to the sheer quantity of men craving straight recreational sex without the emotional side dishes. The great preponderance of men are not tattooed sailors who haven't seen dry land in months but merely ordinary chaps, many of them in 'committed' relationships or happily married, in search of non-verbal but nevertheless highly penetrative relationships. The choice is difficult for there is so much to choose from, and strolling around with an erection adds to the general confusion, making a simple decision hard: which woman to fuck. Smoking the freely available legalised cannabis only serves to make the decision more difficult.

After an exhausting bout of window shopping, the man gravitates toward a particular woman whom he can envisage himself 'doing things to'. He gives her one last cursory inspection before tapping on the door to discuss the financial and penetrative terms on offer. She provides him with the set menu, informing him that 'a suck and fuck is fifty guilders'. He then enquires as to any à la carte dishes on offer and other special items not listed on the menu. Popular requests include: 'extra positions' or being 'sucked without a condom', each of which invite a surcharge of around 25 guilders per erection; being 'sucked without a condom and finishing in my mouth' which, though rarely available, will add another 50 to 100 guilders to the basic price; and anal intercourse with a bullet-proof condom, which, when in season, entails a 50 guilders supplementary charge.*

Client and supplier reach an agreement. The man is invited in, places his order and pays in advance before removing all of his clothes. She clinically bathes his resting penis at the sink basin, though by the time she finishes thirty seconds later, it isn't resting any more. She invites him to lie on a single, thin, firm mattress embedded in what can only be described as a purpose built-in knee-high sex console (curiously unavailable at Habitat or MFI). The mirror clad room is iridescent, a gaudy mixture of ultraviolet and red light which seems utterly conducive to what he is about to experience. She lies on the edge of the bed and strokes his penis whilst leaning over him. Contrary to popular belief, there is little raunchiness or vulgarity about her manner, rather an air of that caring and tender professionalism akin to an aromatherapist. As his penis swells and becomes sufficiently firm, she slides her mouth over it, enveloping it almost entirely in a way his own partner would be unable to do. The feeling is almost indescribable, as wonderful as sliding to and fro in

* Data NOT supplied by the Dutch Tourist Authority.

95

a warm and wet vagina. She maintains a constant smooth, deep motion and begins to gently cup and massage his balls with her hand. Within three or four minutes his balls begin to pulsate rhythmically, and as she continues to squeeze them gently using a milking type motion, drawing out his warm fluid into her mouth, any thoughts of Home seem strangely absent. It is all over in less time than you can say: 'I want to get in touch with my emotions.' He makes pleasant small talk as he dresses, thanks her and kisses her on the cheek, before slipping out the door back onto the busy cobblestone pavement. He will be back in the neighbourhood in a few hours.

It may, to many women, seem quite unnecessary for any reasonable looking man to have to resort to paying for sex which on the whole is much more accessible than it used to be, yet prostitution is a flourishing profession with more patrons than ever. One might assume that a husband may want to do things with a prostitute that his wife would find disagreeable, or that in some way he is acting out a need to degrade women. The reason is, however, rather more mundane, for he is in many cases, merely seeking 'efficient' sex without the debilitating ordeal of having to exert any emotional or communicative effort, or having to contend with someone else who is. An added benefit is the ability to satisfy the insatiable male craving for new partners. Having sex with one hundred women in the same position is far more gratifying than having sex with the same woman but in one hundred different positions. Despite the protestations of men 'in touch with themselves', this, for the majority of representative men, is a fact of life not subject to re-education. For while contemporary man may be well advised to *say* the right thing, you can't change the way he actually *feels*. *The Stepford Wives* struck a chord with many men – and feminists – with good reason.

While this pursuit of intercourse may at first appear somewhat extravagant, it becomes clear upon closer inspection that this is not necessarily the case, when one considers the cost of wooing lay women. Although the idea of quantifying the courting process may seem crude, it does provide an insight into the rational side of male sexual psychology, where pragmatism and logistics feature highly. Whilst a drunken encounter at a party may result in 'same night consummation', such couplings are unpredictable and few and far between. Most men have to rely upon the more traditional route to the bedroom, taking him and his chequebook on a journey through restaurants, pubs and cinemas. London-based Mr Middle-Class will, as a rough guide, have to endure a two-week interview before enjoying the fruits of his labour. He would probably have to invest in: three meals @ £50 (including wine and VAT); additional social lubricant imbibed in wine bar or pub averaging at £12 per visit × 6 visits; two trips to the cinema @ £16 (excluding ice-cream and popcorn); plus taxis, say six journeys @ £8.50=£305.00, not to mention the less quantifiable elements of hangovers, telephone calls, stress, fatigue, loss of productivity and, of course, risk of failure. Pretty sobering statistics. A weekend in Amsterdam, however, will cost Mr Middle-Class: return airfare £70; hotel for two nights @ £23 (including breakfast); subsistence allowance c£80; six × fuck'n'suck set menu @ £17.85=£303.10. Six for the price of one. A bargain which, unlike the previous scenario, will leave him relaxed and well rested, ready to face the busy week ahead and £1.90 better off.

However, the limiting factor which prevents the preponderance of men from relying on prostitution isn't financial, but rather that the experience lacks the authenticity of being physically craved, an aspect essential to achieving the profound experience of a deep biological and spiritual connection. As a man, there is nothing quite like feeling your sperm being 'willed' from your body by another body which blatantly yearns for it with all of the accompanying visceral changes: response and counter-response, an interaction, a *relationship*.

The reason women are not the keen customers in prostitution certainly isn't because they don't like spending, it is because women tend to 'like' the people who fuck them. Moreover, women want to be liked by the people who fuck them. No doubt this reluctance to be sexually predatory can be neatly explained away as the result of centuries of sexual and financial subjugation. However, by explaining the less overt sexuality of women as being the result of conditioning, it relegates them to the status of dogs that were trained inappropriately; the implication being they don't know what they really want and need to be 'educated'. Presumably, intensive courses in sexual empowerment, combined with improved financial circumstances, will redress the balance, thereby liberating women to unleash a backlog of pent-up sexual *chutzpah*. Psychology has been quick to recognise the need to 'educate', with workshops in, for instance, flirting, now being offered. While this strikes many as rather amusing, it is yet another reflection of the consistent attempts to reduce natural human characteristics to manageable components to be reactivated upon demand.

To gain a greater understanding of female sexuality, one need not travel any further than the local library, for it all takes place in a burst of introspection inspired by the printed word. Men's sexual 'imaginations' are easily accommodated with a minimum of text and a predominance of gynaecological close-ups, whereas women's magazines which have attempted to 'rival' this distinctly male approach to sexuality have failed miserably. Mills & Boon, on the other hand, continues to prosper unabated: one Mills & Boon novel sells somewhere in the world every two seconds. In the United States, Harlequin Enterprises Ltd, the American equivalent of Mills & Boon, sells more than 200,000,000 books annually and produces about 70 titles a month. Dedicated readers may go through several books a week. A Harlequin representative believes that: 'Our books give women everything, a loving relationship, commitment and having sex with someone they care about.' Ironically, such novels are occasionally written by a man using a female pen-name, but Harlequin reveals that 'our avid readers can always tell.' No doubt the existence of such a 'servant-girl-fiction' market, once described by George Eliot as 'silly novels by lady novelists', will be dismissed as an artefact of sexual conditioning.

While men are highly responsive to visual stimuli and are easily aroused by the prospect of anonymous sex, women's erotic fantasies are inextricably linked with the emotional: creating the 'right' atmosphere (something a man can achieve simply by closing his eyes and undoing his trousers), having a partner to whom she feels spiritually attached, being attentive toward one another: all the components of the traditional candlelit dinner for two. There is one further subtle difference: she doesn't pay.

Rachael Silver, author of *Where Their Feet Dance: English Women's Sexual Fantasies*, states, for example: 'Women are more prone than men to sexual fantasy because they have been trained by male domination to experience certain types of sex only through their imaginations.' What is highly entertaining, is the in-fighting between the various female media hyenas as to the kind of 'proper' sexual fantasies English women *should* be having. In reviewing Silver's book for the *Sunday Times*, Kate Saunders complains bitterly that the fantasies depicted are simply too ordinary. 'I missed the wild exhilaration of [Nancy] Friday's explosive revelations' [*The Secret Garden*]. 'I reserve my greatest disappointment, however, for the sheer tweeness and banality of some English women's imaginations. . . . Most striking is the reluctance of many of these women even to dream about (or admit that they dream about), anything beyond their own barriers of suitability.' What Saunders appears to find most distasteful are the examples of 'Jennifer' who said that she wouldn't be turned on by a 'big, hunky man walking down the street . . . if he didn't look honest or reliable,' and 'Ursula', whose fantasy consists of a classically romantic scenario involving a beautiful garden and a sixteenth-century paramour.

Like many media women, Ms Saunders finds it difficult to accept that she has little in common with most women. However, she does have company. The writer Sally Beauman seems more at ease with the sex and shopping genre of romance fiction:

The heroines of romance finally began to come clean about their motives . . . not love and marriage but power . . . these heroines were freed both erotically and economically. They chose, and discarded, their own sexual partners . . . they may since have been succeeded by gentler heroines, for whom stacking supermarket shelves is a meaningful gesture of female emancipation . . . they did represent an advance on their earlier, more devious and more subservient sisters.

One gets the feeling that such critics would have few qualms about feeling wistful after reading *Pride and Prejudice*: male interest would, of course, focus more upon the painting of the woman on the front cover.

The dividing line between self-improvement and entertainment is becoming very indistinct. A new breed of female media hyena has emerged in the form of poor fiction writers attempting to redress a perceived imbalance in sexual prowess through the portrayal of women as sexually driven heroines. Miss Elizabeth Bennett has no place here. For instance, Yvonne Roberts's novel, *Every Woman Deserves an Adventure*, is described as: 'Kay, bored with being respectable, responsible, and reliable, infuriated with her husband's infidelity, embarks on a sexual odyssey, intent on proving that the female of the species is equally capable of playing Casanova.' While some women are capable of engaging in modes of behaviour which are traditionally the province of men, most are not, for sex usually brings with it an emotional hangover. This is not a cause for remorse.

Efforts to tutor women to 'play Casanova', when most are not comfortable with this role, deny them their basic nature, which is as oppressive as the previous situation whereby society denied women's sexual needs. Michael Mason, author of *The Making of Victorian Sexual Attitudes*, provides an historical perspective of how women have always viewed 'free love' as exploitation: 'Robert Owen, whose Utopian blueprint banned marriage in favour of open relationships and free love, should have been a hero of sexual liberation but working-class women distrusted his views. They did not want to give up their husbands. To them liberation was repression and they distrusted the motives of men who advocated it.' To pressure women to adopt a sexual posture with less emotional content is as unreasonable as the drive to make men feel as if they should try and associate erections with emotions.

The implications of the above differences between men and women for relationships is unequivocal, and the question, 'why are men so unfaithful?', would be more appropriately phrased, 'why aren't men more unfaithful?'.

However, such implications are never made clear by psychology and, more importantly, the counselling organisations which specialise in dealing with relationship difficulties. Male infidelity comes in many shades of grey and in most cases is likely to be far more superficial and entail less, if any, emotional investment. On the other hand, female infidelity carries with it greater risks to the relationship. Italian husbands, for instance, have a saying: 'Toothbrushes and wives are not to be shared with anybody.' For centuries, the greatest insult to an Italian man has been to call him *'cornuto'*, a man whose wife is being *publicly* unfaithful, causing him to lose face. Even Northern Italian men who, unlike their Southern counterparts, display a less violent reaction to their wives' infidelities, become somewhat more animated if her dalliances become public: image is everything, even in infidelity.

Any notion of parity in sexuality and fidelity is an artificially imposed concept which perpetuates unrealistic expectations and damages relationships unnecessarily. While the field of socio-biology managed successfully to explain clearly the dynamics of fidelity, monogamy and polygamy, based upon genes and hormones, favouritism has recently been shown toward a new field called *evolutionary psychology*. The name itself implies the application of conscious thought to evolutionary behaviour, i.e. sex and relationships. Evolutionary psychology has a more upbeat, positive account of romance and, as such, has been ushered in by psychology and high-profile media, even making the front cover of *Time* magazine. Gene-centred views of the human condition, curiously, never appeared centre-stage. The new view emphasises the role of free-will and the social environment in determining the way we conduct our relationships: genetic and hormone-based behaviour may be *natural* but they are not unchangeable. Moreover, such a Darwinian perspective of natural selection does not work toward the overall social good. Morality is often conceptualised as having to battle with human nature; even Darwin saw humans as the only moral animal species and stated: 'a moral being is one who is capable of comparing his past and future actions or motives, and of approving or disapproving of them.' However, while we may approve or disapprove of certain of our actions or motives, act we will, and this is the modern paradox which is heightened by psychology. Having the ability to subject our lives to examination, self-awareness, memory, foresight and judgement, does

102

not confer upon us the ability to adjust our behaviour to suit our own or anyone else's conclusions.

Those who still cling to a belief in parity within infidelity may be interested in some recent research published in *The Lancet*. Researchers studying the effects of pregnancy appear to have found a biologically sound justification for the greater importance of female fidelity as opposed to male fidelity. The study implies that a woman's body becomes 'attuned' to a man's sperm, whereas her immune system reacts against a new partner. Women who conceive within four months of meeting a new partner are twelve times more likely to suffer from the raised blood pressure condition, pre-eclampsia, during pregnancy than those who conceive after living with a man for more than a year. Furthermore, women who have had previous children, which usually reduces the risk of pre-eclampsia, are still five times more likely to develop pre-eclampsia by changing partners as opposed to remaining with an existing long-term partner.

This is not to say that, after recognising these problematic differences between men and women, women will be able to rationalise infidelity on the part of their male partners; but acknowledging such a disparity is surely a far healthier stance than allowing themselves to believe that things should not, and cannot, be this way. It is nevertheless interesting to see how psychology and counselling organisations accommodate these uncomfortable issues. The answer is, they don't, and in other cases they actually refute them. The next generation is currently being inculcated with such politically derived guidance. The Family Planning Association-backed book *How Sex Works* states definitively: 'Old rules about sexual relationships need not apply today.' They continue in the section entitled 'Treating Girls Differently':

There is one persistent stereotype that most of us recognise, and that won't go away. A boy who boasts about his sexual exploits and has many different sexual partners is regarded as a real man, and one of the lads. On the other hand, a girl who sleeps with a number of different boys is sometimes branded as loose and easy. The message is that girls shouldn't have any sexual desires, or at any rate they shouldn't do anything about them. This is patently unequal treatment and untrue. Most people are a mixture of characteristics, and it is better to view people as individuals than to prejudge them on the basis of sex, race, or class.

While many of the faint-hearted prefer to see libido as a force driven by emotion among other things, basic libido is the product of testosterone, which is as important to women as it is to men in order to have a normal libido. In fact, women who suffer damage to their adrenal gland, which produces and controls the flow of testosterone, experience complete loss of sex drive. The treatment to restore this loss does not involve counselling, rather, testosterone injections. Many menopausal women comment on their declining libido and sexual responsiveness. Studies have found that prescribing small doses of testosterone to post-menopausal women dramatically increased their sexual desire and energy levels while oestrogen replacement had virtually no effect. It was even reported that a few husbands complained that their wives became overly demanding: a late-life insight into role reversal.

It is important to point out that a man's brain is far more responsive to the effects of testosterone and moreover, he has, after puberty, twenty times more of this hormone in his body than a woman. It is also interesting to discover that the time in a woman's menstrual cycle when her libido is most pronounced coincides with the moment that her levels of testosterone are at their peak. Younger women with higher levels of testosterone have been found to become aroused more easily and for longer periods than women with normal levels. Ironically, these hormonally endowed females were having less sex and enjoying it less than normal women. It was suggested that such women tend to be more career-orientated and may therefore be more demanding, or have higher sexual expectations.

RELATE has published a section entitled 'Unequal Libidos – Different Appetites', in their book, *The RELATE Guide to Better Relationships*. RELATE believes that:

Perhaps the most difficult to remedy cause of a troublesome sex life is a discrepancy in libido – your sexual needs are different. Some people are far less interested in sex than their partners, not because of any problem, but because it's the way they are . . . it is important for domestic harmony that you both have roughly the same needs. When there is a genuine imbalance in how much sex you both need, it is necessary to compromise. One of the best ways to do this is to agree when you will make love – say, once a week. To make the agreement work, the one with the higher sex drive must undertake not to ask for sex at any other time. The one with the lower sex drive has to agree to participate fully and willingly on the agreed date. The deal is that he does not make sexual advances at any other times, and she undertakes to participate fully when they do make love. When it is the woman who has the greater sexual appetite the man can feel that his masculinity is threatened.

This point indicates that, typically, RELATE cannot simply accept that a man may not feel in the slightest bit 'threatened', but merely find his partner's libido tiresome, tedious and a terrible nuisance. RELATE must instead invoke a political interpretation to account for it. After all, penises are such political organs and can never be taken at face value.

Given the greater impetus and physicality of a man's sex drive and the fact that he has put aside his craving for new partners to commit himself to a relationship, let us examine the prevailing wisdom of 'unequal libidos', in situ.

When informed by his partner that 'there is a genuine imbalance in how much sex we both need', he agrees to limit sex to 'once a week' and agrees that 'the deal is that he does not make sexual advances at any other times.' Presumably, for the remaining six days of the week, he is expected to carefully consider the option of engaging in a series of (six) deep and meaningful physical relationships – with himself, providing of course that both he and his rapacious appendage can come to a civilised agreement to participate 'fully and willingly on the agreed dates'. His relationship with himself can then progress to the next stage . . . with all the excitement of secret rendezvous (and a locked bathroom door). Conversely, a woman, who as part of the 'agreement' undertakes 'to participate fully and willingly on the agreed date', has her work cut out for her. Glancing at her diary and then conjuring up genuine sexual responsiveness-to-order, goes very much against the nature of female sexuality and can have unfortunate, even painful, consequences for her in the dry form of abrasion due to a lack of genuine enthusiasm.

Such a highly managed approach, which has now become the accepted approach to remedy disparities in libido within a relationship, is remarkably naive and fails to address the central issue: people, even men, don't want their partners merely to agree to have sex, they need their partners to genuinely *want* to have sex. There is, however, one obvious solution which is unlikely to feature highly in any marriage guidance manifesto: in an effort to reconcile his need for more sex and his need to show consideration for his partner by not imposing upon her his own selfish need for physical gratification, the oversexed male partner merely creeps out of the house to seek sex elsewhere. This, by the way, is a standard solution in the *real* world. And there are benefits to be derived for the relationship, for in addition to making him a more amiable and less demanding chap to have around the house, her sixth sense may inadvertently cause her to desire him more.

The disparity between what people *say* turns them on in relationships and what *actually* turns them on is an interesting area to explore. Although it is well documented, scientific studies are quite unnecessary for one to discover that a woman's requirements in her partner, both short- and long-term, are considerably more stringent than a man's, which consistently reflects an emphasis on physical attractiveness. What is most fascinating is the inconsistency in what makes women passionate. One of the greatest examples of this dilemma was played out between a couple I know who live in an area of London known as Stoke Newington. This unlovely part of London nestles between gentrified Islington and Hackney (which vies with Stoke Newington for the higher statistics of crack-dealers per capita). While many people *have* to live in Stoke Newington, there are others who *want* to live there for socio-political reasons. This is a consistent theme among many middle-class people who, in an attempt to maintain their 'political integrity', claim they want to be 'part of the whole community'. With this in mind, they buy up and gentrify older properties which would have been available to the local community on lower incomes. They then set about expressing how 'socially aware' they are by reinforcing the locks and putting bars on the windows. Despite their 'concern' and empathy with this interesting and eclectic community, the only chance the locals ever have to 'pop in', is when the residents are not at home. The couple in question *want* to live in Stoke Newington.

The wife concerned comes from an upper middle-class bohemian, soft-left family. While she may have dallied in working-class boyfriends before she became broody, her husband is hardly a Del-boy, rather, the product of Charterhouse and Oxford. He is a dear and sensitive man, thoughtful, intelligent, kind, considerate and articulate. Having read English, he now teaches the subject and writes poetry. One night, this couple were awoken by noises in the street. Looking out of the window, they saw a member of the local community banging his fists on car roofs and trying the doors. It was obvious from his behaviour that, unlike the husband, this was not a sensitive, thoughtful, intelligent, kind, considerate and articulate man, and he was highly unlikely to have been the product of public school. The next thing they knew, he was banging aggressively on their front door, at which point the wife told her husband to 'do something'. He rolled up his sleeves and dialled 999. Considering his age, 49, and his rather slight stature, this was an eminently sensible course of action. His wife, obviously expecting an eclectic blend of poetry and pugilism, did not agree, complaining privately that she felt disappointed that his response was not 'manly' enough. Such ambivalence is not restricted to doorsteps in Stoke Newington.

In love-making, the disparity between the expressed desire for qualities such as 'being considerate' is often at odds with what actually transpires in bed. Few women would confess openly to being turned on and becoming wetter during sex by having their hair pulled or by being fucked from behind while the man grabs her by the scruff of the neck and forces her head down: but a significant proportion are. Even unmentionable overtures such as squeezing her throat in a pseudo-choking manner make many women breathe faster, but not because they are breathless. While all of these modes of behaviour symbolise male brutality and the oppression of women, what is a modern man to make of this discrepancy in values and apparent desires? Some clarification from the caring world of psychology would be helpful here.

Concepts such as honesty, openness, equality and negotiation have a high profile in the prevailing wisdom on conducting 'improved' relationships. Closer examination, however, begs the question that while such terms have a warm and egalitarian appeal that would make any democratic government smile, to what extent can they be applied indiscriminately to relationships between men and women? The mating game is a prime example of honesty being, at times, a deeply unintelligent policy. To gain a better insight into the applicability of true honesty to achieving intimacy, let us now tune into a radio counselling phone-in:

Doctor: And now we move to Chigwell to speak to Billy. Hello Billy, you're through to the Problem Hour. How can I help you?

Billy: Well, Doc, I don't exactly have a problem, if yer know wot I mean. You see, it's this bird I spotted down the booza. I fink I'm in love wiv 'er, but I dunno 'ow I can get 'er to fancy me. I'm going down the booza again on Saturday night. Wot do yer fink I should do?

Doctor: Well, Billy, I always feel that honesty is the best policy. You see, many women complain nowadays that men are unwilling to get in touch with and express their true emotions; they find it difficult to trust men because men are not always truthful with their feelings. Men often try to put on an act to impress women instead of just being themselves, which is what women really want. Do you hear what I'm saying, Billy?

Billy: Yeah, I fink so Doc.

Doctor: Good. So remember that the best relationships are based on complete and total honesty and communication of your feelings toward the other person. Just be yourself and everything else will work itself out. Do you hear what I'm saying, Billy?

Billy: Sure fing Doc!

Doctor: Good, now give us a ring back on Monday and let us know how you got on. Would you do that for me, Billy?

Billy: Will do Doc!

Monday evening . . .

Doctor: Thanks for ringing back, Billy. How did things go?

Billy: Well Doc, I did like yer said. I wos completely and totally honest wiv 'er and communicated my feelings. I says to 'er, 'Darling, I gotta be honest wiv yer. I fink yer a cracking bird and in order to communicate my deep feelings for yer, I'd really like to give yer a good seeing to from behind, ASAP.'

Doctor: Oh . . . I see.

Billy: Anyways, she says to me, 'Piss off you filfy little bastard.' So I'm not sure what to fink Doc. I dunno if this honesty business has paid off and she's just playing hard to get, or wot?

Doctor: You obviously didn't listen to a word I said.

Billy: But I did. You said to be meself and be honest.

Doctor: Look, haven't you ever read any Barbara Cartland? You see, it's all about romance . . . fantasy if you like. Do you hear what I'm saying, Billy?

Billy: Oh, I get it. So yer wanted me to lie. What didn't yer say so in the first place Doc? It makes fings so much easier.

Lying to a woman can serve a very constructive purpose. If a man is genuinely interested in a woman, in terms of a possible long-term relationship, he realises that one of the quickest ways of getting his foot into her emotional doorway, thereby enabling him to plead his case from a much stronger vantage point, is to simply sleep with her. However, he also realises that, by openly telling her that he wants to sleep with her straight away, because he finds her so overwhelmingly attractive and desirable in every way, karma and all, he will be less likely to be doing so in the near future. Instead, he says and does whatever is necessary to reach that emotional and physical vantage point, that very evening if at all possible, his intentions being wholly honourable. Men do have some redeeming features.

Of course, if the same man only wants a one-night stand, he'll need to employ the same tactics.

Equality and negotiation: terms normally reserved for political resolutions, have found their way into the psychology of relationships. It is now generally believed that the distribution of power within a relationship should, in a general sense, be equal. In addition to sparing the less powerful partner any feelings of entrapment and oppression within a relationship, making a concerted effort to achieve and maintain equality is thought to be conducive to greater continuity and equilibrium. Most acknowledge that it is difficult to quantify power and equality in any specific sense and that, throughout a relationship, power is often a somewhat pendulous phenomenon, with men and women retaining and wielding power in different spheres, in different ways and at different times. However, as is the case with many other concepts found within psychology, notions of 'power-sharing' are yet another unnatural and externally derived construct. People have little interest in sharing their perceived power within a relationship; this is particularly so for men, for the reasons discussed in the last chapter. Moreover, men on the whole feel intuitively that there is no better position to negotiate from than a position of strength, and suffer little discomfort at the prospect of having relationships on their own terms. Relationships are not and never will be about emotional parity, nor are they about 'rights', rather, they constitute the satisfying of complementary needs and roles.

Part of empowering oneself and raising self-esteem involves meeting people and initiating relationships. This endeavour is not merely a matter of maximising the number of potential partners one might meet, but also involves a consideration for the way one reacts both verbally and non-verbally to others on a day-to-day basis. Given the current climate, such interactions are fraught with difficulties, misinterpretations and embarrassment.

Psychologists are not exempt from such awkward ordeals:

Being the eldest of five boys, with the dog and even the pet baby alligator being male, there was little room for female role modelling in my house. Not being surrounded by women, I had less early experience in 'reading' them. This in turn left me with a diminished ability to notice women who displayed an interest in me. Such imperviousness has meant that they have had to make their intentions known in rather less subtle ways in order for me to register their interest. The thought of the possibility of missed opportunities due to my social blindness is, of course, today a source of deep regret and bitter self-recrimination.

It is with this predisposition that I came to meet a female producer for the recording of a brief radio programme. When she greeted me, I saw her Eighties' shoulderpads, business woman's shirt and clipboard, and while I found her pretty, there was something about her professional veneer, and that didn't send tingles up my spine. At the end of the day, I shook her hand, we said goodbye, and although I enjoyed working with her, I didn't think much more about it. We had occasion to work together subsequently and I got to know her better. There was an air of familiarity about her, she reminded me of the proverbial 'girl next door', with freckles and big green eyes – the younger sister of a boy I might have played with when I was little: she had also spent some of her childhood in America, which may have heightened this sense of camaraderie, maybe even déjà vu. She was highly intelligent and had a somewhat scientific perspective which I, being a scientist myself, found very appealing. I, in a strange way, began to feel close to her, not in an obvious sexual sense, in fact, not being 'in touch with my emotions', I wasn't sure what I felt: a familial warmth of the kind that exists between a long-lost brother and sister who rediscover one another; or the protective feelings of a father toward a lost child? A deep affection bordering on romance: there was certainly the uncanny feeling that we had known one another for a long time, the sort of feeling you get at the beginning of a deep friendship.

None of this was helped by her habit of looking at me

with a piercing gaze when we spoke, which at times I found disconcerting to the point of breaking off eye-contact out of sheer abashment. After all, we were only 'work mates' and she did have a boyfriend, a fact which in itself added a further ambiguity to the situation. For on two occasions, when we were telling each other about our lives, she commented that her boyfriend was quite a straight, conventional type of man, and although she described him as self-assured, safe and monogamous, I got the distinct impression that her relationship lacked any element of danger, eccentricity or unpredictability. She also joked that she hoped he wouldn't ask her to marry him – because she'd have to say 'no'. At this point, my perceptions were, for the most part, subliminal.

Despite my inability to pick up signals, I began to feel that, maybe, she was testing the waters to see if there was a possibility of us becoming more than just good chums. Once we were no longer working together, a couple of months passed without us seeing each other, then she and I arranged to get together for lunch. On the day we were due to meet, she rang and suggested we also go to the cinema. There was a certain clumsiness about the way things went that day, as if both of us were preoccupied. It was at this point that I became aware of a growing sense of ambivalence and I thought it best to define our relationship in some way. A few days later, I rang her and suggested we get together soon. She said she was unavailable for a couple of weeks and would be in touch. On a warm, sunny day she rang and suggested we go somewhere nice. When I opened the door to greet her, she gave me a big hug. We then drove to Kew Gardens where we walked around, being casually familiar and quite playful with each other. Then she suggested we find a place under a tree to rest; we did this, and while I sat up against the trunk, she lay on the ground, looking up at the canopy. She closed her eyes and asked me to listen to the sound of the leaves

114

rustling in the wind. Not the kind of thing to suggest to your dustman. It was at this point that I felt most confused about her intentions: were they horticultural or otherwise? Did she expect me to say or do something romantic? I have had many platonic and professional relationships with women, but none of these had resembled anything like this, nor prepared me for how to deal with it. And Desmond Morris wasn't available for comment.

I was too embarrassed to broach the subject, and let the moment pass. However, at dinner that night I knew I had to say something. I may be a psychologist, but I also have the right to be a repressed man. By the time we had finished pudding, I still hadn't been able to introduce the subject into conversation. Fate, however, was on my side and while she recounted a story over coffee, she happened to mention that some of her friends said she used to behave in a flirtatious manner. I waded in with both feet and, with the predictability of a soap opera writer, said: 'It's funny you should mention that, because sometimes when you gaze at me, I wonder what you really mean.' She replied: 'What do *you* mean by that?' I added: 'It isn't just the looks, but some of the things you said about your boyfriend being a bit boring made me wonder whether you're unfulfilled in some way . . .' What I meant was, emotionally and romantically unfulfilled, not sexually. Unfortunately, she didn't see it that way, turning red in the face. Her reaction vacillated between irritation, consternation, embarrassment, surprise and bewilderment. She made it very clear that she could not envisage herself being without her boyfriend and couldn't imagine that she would have intentionally said anything against him. Her responses only confirmed my belief that my reluctance to discuss emotional issues may not have been such a bad thing after all.

Anyway, I took her at her word, acknowledging that this was obviously a bad case of crossed-wires and, being convinced that

115

she had only ever wanted to be good chums, I launched into 'chummy' behaviour, which between men means talking about myself in terms of work and sex life, especially my sex life. In fact, in order to reassure her that I had been happy to be chums all along, I moaned about the emotional aggravation caused by just wanting to have easy-going sex with women: the very subject I often discuss with my male friends. No sooner had I calmed the previous upset, than I started a new one, for she replied sarcastically: 'Well if that's what you were hoping for with me, I'm sorry to have disappointed you.'

Psychology has encouraged the idea of men and women being pally in the same way that they can with people of their own sex. However, serious consideration must be given to realistic consequences of this assumption. While it may in theory be a perfectly reasonable aspiration for a woman to want to be considered 'one of the boys', the reality is that there is a certain time frame and decorum that must generally be observed in order to avoid the above scenario. This experience highlights the need for clarification in what behaviour constitutes professional versus platonic versus romantic or sexual intent. Those involved in legislation concerning sexual harassment have had to grapple with these issues; those involved in self-improvement and empowerment need to take a close look at the fine detail of their general recommendations. Once social norms pertaining to the behaviour exhibited by men and women toward one another begin to be discounted, chaos ensues. Relativism is a very naive position to adopt when considering the way that men and women conduct themselves. Though it may seem rather prescriptive, social rules exist in every society and for good reason.

There has also been much discussion of how women can empower themselves to initiate relationships with men. Central to this lies the basic question about making the proverbial 'first move'. While there are those who claim that men are intimidated by such overtures, the situation isn't as simple as it is made out to be. Given that males focus upon the importance of physical attractiveness in a prospective partner, women must be realistic in ensuring that they know their own level of appeal. However, even this assessment is fraught with problems because women are notoriously inexpert at gauging their own desirability, often focusing almost exclusively on qualities such as the size of their bottoms and the cellulite imprinted thereon. They often overlook rather more subtle factors such as a coquettish demeanour which can drive men wild. Moreover, they must of course first try to ascertain whether the object of their desire appears in any way interested in them. Women who are quite certain that their feelings are reciprocated may be well advised to make a direct overture. Those who are in any way unsure are still in a rather strong position and with the added advantage of having a ladder to climb down: transmitting the obvious, yet traditional, signals of interest will usually prompt a response if there is sufficient interest and will spare both parties significant embarrassment if there is not.

Being sexually empowered does not mean trying to be 'one of the boys'. As much as men may publicly lament the fact that women always expect them to associate sex with emotion, women who openly objectify sex before a prospective partner may be doing themselves a 'disservicing'. While such provisos are usually attributed to a male fear of emasculation, it is actually more straightforward than that. Predatory behaviour and discussing and joking about sex in a detached manner may make for interesting conversation but will ultimately be perceived by most men as a characteristic associated with their gender. Be it fair or not, men define women as associating sex with emotion and caring: attempts to convince them otherwise may result in a woman being labelled 'chum' and men don't sleep with their chums. Again, it is that sense of otherness that creates attraction. Social norms apply to women who would like to end up in bed with a particular man. These basic behaviours may be trivialised by being described as a product of social conditioning. They are not.

And so to bed.

6: Penetrating Sex

Sex was at one time guided by instinct. However, such guidance is now offered in a much wider variety of forms. A natural, instinctive part of life has become the province of 'experts' who advise us how best to conduct our exchanges of grunts, now referred to as 'physical relationships' or 'sexual encounters'. The search for sexual gratification is reflected in all aspects of the media and is catered for by psychologists, psychiatrists and major counselling organisations. We are urged to think of sex as an entity to be controlled and refined: a form of 'planned' spontaneity, where orgasms are divided equally, and letting it all hang out, in the form of American cinema-style moaning and groaning, is interspersed with polite requests for 'fellatio' and glasses of *Aqua Libra*. All of this to be followed by a ten-minute rendition of 'How Was It For You Dear?'. Those who appear reluctant to engage in such post-orgasmic introspection are considered 'uptight' because they have 'hang-ups' (or they're asleep).

Sex used to be 'the most fun you can have without laughing', but now it's just something you have without laughing. Object-ifying sex has, in many ways, been terribly counter-productive. Like the comedian Tony Hancock, who, after trying to analyse the success of his humour, ceased to be funny, too much sexual soul-searching can ruin a normally reflexive experience.

Psychology has again confused the ability to understand 'how sex works' with the idea of trying harder to make it work for you. Those involved in psycho-sexual work argue that the public still lacks sufficient knowledge when it comes to sex and that it is therefore necessary to examine and discuss it in order to overcome this 'deficiency'. It is easy, however, to forget that young teenagers who live in institutions for the mentally retarded have to be protected from pregnancy because they know intuitively how to have sex. Moreover, few animals need to be told what to do or how to do it, and although humans must consider the element of mutual pleasuring, this is also something which is intuitive. This precludes the necessity for 'guidance' and the industry based around this assumption. Such an industry has served to both create and then deal with the unrealistic expectations they have encouraged. Erroneous ideas concerning the 'successful' sex lives of others are reinforced by media portrayals of glamorous married couples still smitten with lust for one another after 'all these years'. Ironically, the most unlikely bedfellows are actually marriage and sex, yet this is precisely where much confusion resides. This is also where the greatest opportunities for 'intervention' rest. In point of fact, burning sex stems from all of the ingredients that can work against marriages: excitement, mystery, unreliability and tension. One is given to believe that the flame of passion can be continually rekindled. However, as Chris D'Souza put it: 'Injecting passion into a passionless marriage is rather like trying to heat up an omelette: it cannot be done.'

RELATE is a prime example of commercial misguidance. To draw attention once again to *The RELATE Guide to Sex in Loving Relationships* which states: 'As RELATE knows from over fifty years of working with couples, you can make a bad sex life good, and a good sex life even better. This book shows you how to . . . create a sex life that is tailor-made for your relationship alone. Step-by-step [it] shows you how to . . . draw up your own "better sex" plan.' When referring to sex, RELATE feels that 'just because it is natural doesn't mean that it is simple . . . To use words is natural, but to become an articulate adult involves work, education and practice. Sex is similar . . . and

120

it [good sex] doesn't just happen . . . although we may know many of the ingredients, we might not know the essential recipe.' Their wisdom continues: 'Sex in a loving relationship is better than sex without love.' This may be a truism for many women. Would it not be more honest to suggest that sex in a loving relationship may certainly be more socially desirable and convenient? To state definitively that sex in a loving relationship actually feels better, is politically motivated positive thinking. There is an obsession in trying to link sex and love that is not restricted to the sex education classes in state schools. Given the large proportion of Cabinet ministers caught with their trousers down whilst drawing up their own 'better sex' plan, one suspects that sex in a loving relationship is not necessarily 'better'. It is interesting to note that to date, there have been no equivalent female resignations.

The Family Planning Association-backed book, *How Sex Works*, informs young people about 'Reaching Orgasm': 'Although org-asms are important to most people, they are not the only sexual sensation – there are plenty of others to enjoy . . . foreplay, for example, can be continued until orgasm . . . It can be as enjoyable as intercourse . . .' The Health Education Authority's book, *Your Pocket Guide to Sex*, declares confidently: 'Penetration isn't essential. And neither is coming.' It then goes on to dismiss erections: 'A big, hard dick does not a good lover make.' The Terrence Higgins Trust guides women with the advice: 'Fortunately, there are lots of ways to make sex fun, enjoyable and safe. Some of these are listed below . . .' The 'list' includes such hot activities as 'Talking about sex and sharing fantasies' (No. 3 on the list); 'Massage, hugging and cuddling' (No. 5); 'Showering together' (No. 6); 'Deep kissing (snogging or French kissing)' (No. 9); 'Patting and spanking (but not so hard you draw blood)' (No. 10), finally to arrive at 'Vaginal penetration', which of course could never be allocated a prominent position on the scale of enjoyment, so it is safely placed at number 11, just before 'Anal penetration'. The same ideas are reiterated several pages later: 'There are countless alternatives to penetrative sex such as massage, nibbling, fingering, rubbing, sharing fantasies, cuddling, stroking and licking. . . . Using your imagination will make it enjoyable, fun, playful and sexy! So if your partner sees safer sex as imposing a set of restrictions rather than possibilities, you can set him or her straight!'

All of the above statements about non-penetrative sex are nowadays accepted without question. A concerted effort is being made to convince people that the entire basis of sex can be *changed* merely by redefining what was previously considered foreplay – to now be thought of as full-blown 'sex'. Penetration is considered a somewhat male way to view sex, being 'phallocentric': such a view takes no account of the fact that even though many women may come more easily through other means, and that men too adore all of the various accompaniments, penetrative sex results in a feeling of genuine union. Penetration leads to a level of intimacy that all of the non-penetrative sessions in the world cannot achieve. Given that penetrative sex is at the very least an artefact of the reproductive act – the issuing of genetic instructions – the emotional consequences must be more profound than its pale imitations. Part of the reason may lie in the fact that a woman has literally opened herself up in a way that renders her more vulnerable than she would be in any other situation and men unknowingly sense this heady combination of trust and vulnerability, which creates the essence of human bonding: 'I may be a strong woman, but by allowing you inside me, I'm placing myself entirely in your hands.' Despite modern contraceptive technology, the mind, at a much deeper level, does still respond to sex as the 'real thing', the reproductive act. It is therefore ironic to find that while the authorities try so desperately to link sex and emotional intimacy, they overlook this short-cut. Deep penetration can convey more than words could ever say: it is not an 'option' to be selected from a menu of offerings.

RELATE is concerned 'by men talking to each other about sex who routinely exaggerate and boast. They rarely say (truthful) things', while the Health Education Authority believes that 'Women are more honest.' This attitude, combined with a jaundiced view of deep penetration, is indicative of the guileful stance taken toward male sexuality, which is generally not thought of as being as 'correct' and therefore not as worthy as female sexuality. No doubt if men were willing to exchange their overriding concern with deep penetration and sperm squirting, for soft caresses, stroking and fondling, they would be duly patted on the head by the 'relationship establishment'. Thrusting, penetrating, a greater sense of immediacy which manifests itself in badly wanting to come – all to be 'reduced' to braggadocio in full earshot of other men the next day while there's still a wet patch on the bed – are, according to such thinking, qualities that need to be better controlled and *changed*. Like 'the male ego', bragging is seen as a 'symptom' of something involving inadequacy: it is, however, merely a symptom of being male. Men do tell one another about the little pleasures in life that make them happy, and despite chronic attempts to attribute ulterior motives, including inadequacies, to such male behaviour, there are no deep underlying motives behind their graphic descriptions of their sexual exploits. However, it is rather convenient to perpetuate the popular myth that bragging is a direct symptom of sexual insecurity or of an 'inferiority complex'. It will no doubt be most disconcerting to some to think that bragging is actually a form of 'male bonding', 'communication' and 'getting in touch with emotions', the 'sharing of true joy': the very emotional experiences which psychology has wanted men to engage in for some time now.

123

The self-appointed, 'well intentioned' interpreters of the male condition, and therefore of the bragging characteristic, make the error of believing that men are somehow deep. This has had the unfortunate effect of leading people to view such boasting as being consciously degrading to women, objectifying their bodies in the way that one would an inanimate sperm receptacle: but like it or not we are sex objects first and intellectuals only secondarily. Deriding sperm receptacles is an insult to sperm and to women. Such interpreters have foolishly helped to create the very feelings of disrespect that they are falsely accusing men of expressing: in fact, misogyny has been a most fertile field to cultivate as of late. Books with titles such as Joan Smith's *Misogynies* are intended to help women by pointing out the various forms of omnipresent male injustice and cruelty toward them, in case they weren't already aware of these. *Misogynies* is described in the publisher's view as the book that 'grapples with the hidden passion that distorts human relations – woman-hating'. Our society now unquestioningly embraces the idea that half of the world's population instinctively hates the other half, as exemplified by the *Listener*'s verdict, cited on the front cover of the book: 'Essential reading . . . leaves you unable to stop thinking of more examples [of misogyny].' The back cover contains the considered judgement of that most divine example of broadsheet impartiality, the *Guardian*: 'It is a fine and invigorating achievement.' No doubt a most useful reference book for overcoming optimism.

It is interesting to note that the term misogyny: 'a morbid hatred of women, an extreme mental state with many possible causes' (*The Wordsworth Dictionary of Sex*) has, according to most dictionaries, no direct antonym, but curiously, the *Chambers' Thesaurus* suggests 'feminist' as the closest one can get. Men may be negligent, 'phallocentric' and more insensitive and selfish than women; they may find women alien or possibly even fear them, but they certainly do not *dislike* or *hate* women as a sex. Therefore a more appropriate term would be *misogamy*: 'a morbid hatred of marriage based in many cases on a fear of sexual intimacy or inability to undertake the responsibilities of married life' (*The Wordsworth Dictionary of Sex*) — the nature of the beast, not a psychological disorder. If one wants to initiate a discussion about those who really dislike women, one need look no further than the women in control of the public image of women: magazine editors, picture editors, not to mention the Queen Bee bosses.

One of the 'symptoms' that indicates that one is a 'misogynist' is a marked antipathy toward wearing condoms. No one can be unaware of the concerted effort in recent years to convince the public that if they must have a penetrative relationship, it will feel just as good *with* a condom as without. For example, the Family Planning Association's book *How Sex Works*, in its section entitled 'Condoms', fails to address the issue of loss of sensitivity and makes a blatant attempt to lead the reader to the wrong conclusion by providing a 'real' quote from 'Nathan, 17 years', who informs us: 'All my friends said wearing a condom reduced sensitivity. But when I tried one, it felt okay. I also think it made me last longer.' It is interesting that a more balanced quote wasn't put forward as well; perhaps something along the lines of: 'All the adverts said wearing a condom doesn't affect sensitivity, but when I tried one, I couldn't come, and in the end I lost my erection because I couldn't feel anything — it was like wearing a shell suit.' The Terrence Higgins Trust predictably fails to show any concerns on the part of the man for a loss of sensitivity, but what is most extraordinary is that there is no mention in their booklet, which is specifically aimed at women, of how women themselves feel about condoms and their own sensitivity.

The unmentionable aspect of wearing a condom is that it

isn't just *physical* sensitivity that is affected, but emotional sensitivity as well. There is something about the contact with naked flesh that provides a unique physical and emotional 'connectedness'. How would most people feel at having their face lovingly caressed by someone wearing rubber gloves? While it is often thought that men are the ones who selfishly benefit from not wearing a condom, there are countless women who decide half-way through intercourse that they would prefer to continue without a piece of rubber in the way of their intimacy. Worse still, there is nothing like the feeling of two lots of body fluids mixing inside: Mother Nature wouldn't have it any other way. The obvious attempts to 're-educate' the public to believe otherwise insults one's intelligence. Lying to the public about the 'condom experience' is not the way to encourage safer sex. Honesty should be a pre-requisite to discussing this issue.

And the fallacious ideas continue. The United States has given the world many things, including the cinematic orgasm which was catapulted into public recognition through American film and television. The Americans have, in addition to this, provided us with the appropriate dialogue to precede, accompany, and follow, the orgasm. This has even been reflected by the British Government in its Health Education Authority's 'Pocket Guide to Sex': *Talking about sex before it happens; Talking about sex while you're doing it; How to talk dirty; Talking dirty to each other; Talking dirty amongst yourselves.* If such banter is appreciated, there is a section entitled *Orgasm talk*; and for those who can't be in the same place at the same time, *Telephone Sex* affords one the opportunity to say 'I'm coming'; while for those who are lost for words, there is guidance on 'moans, whimpers, sighs and squeals'. The Terrence Higgins Trust adopts many of the key phrases of self-help psychology in telling women about *'Sexual negotiation – some helpful guidelines'*:

Language for discussing this area is important. . . . One easy way of finding an acceptable language is for both of you to separately say or write down words you are happy with and words you don't like. Then you can sort out which you are prepared to use. Using positive phrases, such as 'I really like . . .', rather than negative lines like 'you don't do it the way that I like . . .', will improve your chance of having a productive dialogue.

The American ideas are continued in the section entitled *'If I discuss safer sex my partner will leave me for someone else'* where it is suggested that 'Assertiveness training may help . . .'

A woman in a long-term relationship is told by the Terrence Higgins Trust that it will actually *improve* the quality of her relationship to inform her long-term boyfriend that he must suddenly adopt a series of new safer sex practices to replace the old ones. The language of American psychology is appropriated to convince her, together with her soon-to-be-perplexed boyfriend, of the benefits: 'Keeping a relationship alive needs an open and honest dialogue. Introducing the subject of safer sex can be part of this process. Explain that as you know more about HIV, you no longer want to risk unsafe sex and that you see safer sex as a way of taking care of each other.' It would be interesting to be a fly on the wall while this advice is implemented:

Soon-to-be-perplexed boyfriend with erection: Gngh! Gngh! Gngh!

Empowered girlfriend (EG):   Kevin, I've got this nifty little leaflet about sex, and now that I know more about AIDS, I no longer want to risk unsafe sex with you. It also says that safer sex is a really good way of taking care of each other. It can keep our relationship alive because it means we can have an open and honest dialogue. Look, it says that here . . .

Perplexed boyfriend with erection: What do you mean, Tina?

EG: Well, if you put on this extra safe condom, which has been approved by the British Standards and the Islington Women's Empowerment Centre, it will help keep both us and our relationship alive. It's part of the process of being open and honest.

Perplexed boyfriend: What are you going on about? We've been doing it for four years, girl! You calling me a poofter or something?

EG: No, no of course not, Kevin. It's just the sensible thing to do these days. It says so on the telly: it's all about trust.

PB: Don't you trust me then?

EG: No, I mean yes. Oh, you know what I mean. It's a sign of our mutual trust that we can do it with a condom on. This other book says it's actually *better* if you use one. Go on, put it on. Just for me?

PB: Oh all right, if it means that much to you.

45 minutes later . . .

EG: What's the matter, Kevin? I thought you fancied me.

128

PB: It's this bloody johnny, Tina. I can't get it up because I can't feel anything.

EG: No. It's because you don't love me any more, isn't it?

PB: Well at least you can't say we didn't have safer sex, can you?

EG: Oh sod this, I'm going down the shops for some chocolate. Do you want anything?

While terms such as 'open and honest', 'dialogue', and 'taking care of each other' are of course the bread and butter of a good loving relationship, hijacking these appealing terms to socially engineer a major public sexual overhaul in the name of 'concern' for 'the public good' is itself not particularly 'open and honest'.

The pressure to make verbal and conscious what is blissfully intuitive can be a most successful way to kill the magic. Statements such as: 'tell me what you want me to do' sound like 'may I take your order?' and are often met with the thought: 'well if you don't bloody know by using your own initiative, I'm not going to bother telling you.' 'Left a bit . . . Right a bit' can be reminiscent of evening classes in ballroom dancing. Furthermore, people like to feel as if their co-fornicator is *driven* to 'do something' intuitively; even if what they're doing is not ideal, the sheer fact that they're *compelled* to act in this way, is a turn-on in itself. Being asked what one would like, makes the experience appear contrived and can place an unwanted momentary responsibility upon someone who is striving to relinquish control and would, quite frankly, rather not have to make any sudden decisions.

The new pressure to 'communicate more with your partner

and let them know what your sexual likes and needs are', is a remarkably naive recommendation advanced by 'experts' ad nauseam. Few people are versed in the kind of language they should use to discuss their most vulnerable and intimate side, and to suddenly parrot these words can be terribly awkward and embarrassing. People are concerned about appearing to be naive, maladroit and inexpert: this is particularly true of men, for while there are public claims that women prefer their men to be sensitive, the unpleasant truth is they don't want their men to be *sexually* sensitive. Men who consult, confer and consider may be applauded within the pages of *Cosmopolitan* and the confines of high-street feminism, but they are not welcome in bed.

Women are not exempt from such psychology-induced dilemmas either. A woman who assertively and directly communicates exactly what turns her on, may run the risk of undermining her partner's sexual confidence by leading him to believe that she is in a somewhat well-informed position, being able to judge and compare him with past lovers: the perfect recipe for ensuring an unintended non-penetrative relationship that evening. Men, who are by nature more competitive, are more vulnerable to such fears and, worse still, their vulnerability can reach flaccid proportions. And so double standards persist in terms of levels of experience perceived to be high, this being considered intimidating by men. While men obviously like their partners to be highly responsive, there is a fine line between this and being too demanding. Moreover, while vulnerability is a quality which men find very attractive in women, the reverse simply isn't true. If it were, then men could afford to feel more comfortable with sexually assertive and experienced women. Sexual communication is like humour – it's the way you tell 'em.

After reading or listening to psychologists and counsellors

discussing sex, one can be forgiven for suspecting that such rational types are themselves rarely impassioned: armchair intercoursers. There are, however, psychologists who step out of the laboratory from time to time in order to conduct field studies. As an American coming out of the Woodstock generation, I was brought up to believe that sex was a natural activity and that women wanted to be spoken to with respect: 'verbal abuse' was terribly uncool. However, I was soon to be enlightened and began to discover the many provisos to this general principle. During my childhood, Julie Andrews was probably the closest I came to a symbol of British femininity: upon my arrival in Britain it came to my attention that British women could not be further from Mary Poppins. On reflection, I would have been better prepared for the British Sexual Experience if I had been exposed to a season of Carry On films: in any event, I had never heard of Barbara Windsor nor for that matter seen a Matron's uniform before. For when it came to British sex, there was, on occasion, the issue of fishnet stockings, suspender belts, leather boots and even suggestions of schoolgirls' uniforms – all of which I found culturally interesting, but which merely represented yet another piece of clothing to be removed in the process of uncontrived sex. There was at times, talk of 'role play' involving 'discipline', 'correction' and lots of spanking. Worst of all, there were occasional requests for the very type of 'verbal abuse' that I was so heavily conditioned never to think of, let alone say. When recounting these 'problems' to English friends of mine who had been to boarding school, I was somewhat surprised that they seemed rather less than sympathetic toward my 'dilemma'. There was one particular situation that stands out and exemplifies everything there is to say about British sexual culture and how saying it with words can be nothing more than an intrusion into an otherwise good fuck. A woman I was seeing continually complained about our communication problems in bed . . .

Bed: Squeak squeak squeak.

Woman: Talk dirty to me.

Me: Shut up, I don't like talking that way to a woman I respect.

Woman: That's not what I mean. Say something really filthy.

Me: Um, um, um.

Bed: Squeak squeak squeak.

Woman: Go on, say something.

Me: Um, um, um. I can't think of anything.

Woman: Call me a nasty little scrubber.

Me: Oh, do I have to?

Bed: Squeak squeak.

Woman: Oh go on, *please*. Call me a filthy little tart.

Me: But I like you!

Woman: Then call me it!

Me: Oh all right. 'You filthy little tart, you.'

Woman: Yes, that's it. Now say it as though you mean it.

Bed: Squeak.

Me: You're a nasty, filthy little nasty tart. How's that?

Woman: More!

Me: Um.

Bed:

Woman: If you *really* cared about me, you'd be more disrespectful.

Me: But apart from that, how was it for you?

Woman: Bastard.

Me: Don't you call me a bastard, you fucking bitch!

Woman: You can't talk to me like that. Get out!

The trend toward greater sexual openness and honesty through the use of language has also been accompanied by higher electricity bills. For some time now, there has been a rather strange idea that making love with the lights on is a display of sexual honesty, openness and confidence. Those that prefer the dark are considered prudish, presumably ashamed of their bodies and what their bodies are doing. However, the assumption that sex is a visual activity is flawed. For vision can actually distract and therefore detract from the sensations which are most central to a sexual experience: touch (kinaesthetic), sound (aural), taste (gustatory) and smell, including pheromones (olfactory); surely enough to contend with without watching the meter go round too. Moreover, vision is the dominant sense and therefore, once it is allowed to enter the sexual arena, it can cause an imbalance. Why do people close their eyes when they kiss? Darkness heightens other sensations – you don't need Stevie Wonder to tell you that – and far from being an indication of inhibition, darkness can generate intense levels of uninhibited physical and emotional passion.

Another sexual misconception occurs in the kitchen. While men simply eat food – women seem to have a relationship with food. Yet, because food, like sex, is one of life's pleasures and necessities, it is continually misappropriated and introduced into conceptions of sex. Even RELATE, not known for its cookery books, lapses into culinary lingo when addressing the issue of achieving 'sensational' sex: 'Sex therapists compare it to food. An experience that includes hours of exciting, exquisitely pleasurable love-play, which leaves you physically drained and satisfied and emotionally loving and close, is the sexual equivalent of a gourmet banquet. It is just not possible to have this experience more than very occasionally and without the planning, preparation and sheer time it involves.' It is this last sentence which is most disconcerting, for it reiterates the notion of planned spontaneity: 'working hard' to 'achieve' 'quality sex'. That aside, like the over-emphasis of vision in sex, adding food to the equation can create competing sensations and in this case, more is not better. Nevertheless, the marriage of food and sex has now become an image which appears in various guises throughout many visual artforms, with advertisements typically featuring images of the latest cuisine being delicately savoured by fashion models. In their ceaseless quest for novelty, the advertising industry, hardly preoccupied with the nation's physical and emotional well-being, has created yet another permutation of sensation by placing ice-cream and sex in bed together. Emphasising to women the endless ways that food can be used either to feel more sensual and/or to include within the 'sexual experience' seems to add insult to injury, considering the relentless pressure women are under to be slimmer. It is obvious to any ass that a delicious candlelit dinner for two can be conducive to romance and that feeding each other is part of 'love play', but taking the food link any more seriously is rather sad. Whipped cream belongs in the fridge, and besides it's high in cholesterol.

The rather frenzied pursuit of 'achieving' female orgasms may either have been tempered slightly, or has merely taken a different form. However, there are still 'orgasm workshops', books, and therapists who assist women in their quest for their share of sexual entitlement and confirmation of their sexuality. It is none the less interesting to see how, through a frivolous medium, the received wisdom of new sexual insights originates and is then disseminated within thousands of dentists' waiting rooms throughout the land: the printed version of what was at one time the province of gossip and rumour in the playground, but this time with less accuracy. In the last couple of years, attention has shifted from the mere clitoral orgasm to the more profound 'vaginal orgasm' with talk of 'G-Spots' only to arrive at discussion in the magazine *Cosmopolitan* of 'female ejaculation', a topic, we are told, which 'still plunges countless women into a helpless state of abject embarrassment'. In the name of 'equality', readers are reassured that: 'Evidence is now emerging that the differences between women's and men's sexual organs are not nearly as great as appearances first suggest.' Scientific substantiation oozes forth with: '*Fact* . . . around the world

135

millions, yes millions, of women produce copious amounts of love juice at orgasm . . . For some, this literally floods out . . . For others, orgasm is even more dramatic, resulting in a spurt of fluid that can travel almost a metre from the body.' The revelations continue, ranging from the case of a woman 'for whom it only happens once every 10 to 15 times' to the woman who collected half a tumbler's worth (to explain to herself the quite astonishing perimeter of the post-coital wet patch).

The magazine is grateful for 'the dawn of contemporary sex-ology' which has enabled a serious discussion of this mysterious phenomenon to arise. Few people, however, seem to question the validity of the term 'sexology': they should, because it is a self-invented term. Nevertheless, full validation is granted to their discussion: 'Now that female ejaculation is medically recognised, if it happens to you, you can at last discuss it with your friends or your lover. And who knows, before long, with total strangers at dinner parties.' The question is posed: 'Does female ejaculation make sex better? And should men swallow it?' A clear answer is never given, or perhaps, being a women's magazine after all, it appears in the Food and Drink section.

While it may indeed be true that some women do ejaculate, it is the motivation and tone of the exposure of such generous new sexual insights that epitomise the difference between helping women feel more comfortable with their sexual side and merely raising performance concerns. The acquisitive tone of attempts to quantify pleasuring, characterises much of this medium's portrayal of sex and at least plants the seed of doubt as to whether one is getting everything one can from this 'hot activity' – entitlement to your sexual 'rights'. As RELATE says: 'When you are in a loving and committed relationship, you deserve to have a sex life that is equally good and satisfying.' Sexual pleasure, however unfair it may seem, is not based upon what people 'deserve'. Such attempts at empowering women in the privacy of their own bedrooms have fallen into the same trap as some attempts at empowering women in the workplace – unwittingly adopting a masculine perspective which doesn't really suit their emotional requirements. Another reflection of the confusion between equality and equivalence which has now led women to experience performance concerns of their own. Conspicuous consumption has permeated the most intimate aspects of human communication and now more women want to be 'good at it' or 'even better'.

Sex, for women in particular, is terribly contextual. Questions as to how intimate an experience is emotionally and physically, or how close one feels to the other person while being fucked, do not make for provocative survey results and accompanying articles. And despite the fact that most people claim they read such 'literature' only half seriously, the subliminal effect on one's expectations can be cumulative. This may not have been so, had these books and articles not been presented as based upon 'sex research', much of it actually conducted by the magazines themselves or authoresses who carry out their poorly designed 'research' with foregone conclusions (and book sales) in mind before the books are even commissioned. All a form of false validation.

What continues to underlay public discussion of 'the female orgasm', or the lack of it, is an almost complete lack of acknowledgement of the fact that, unlike men, women are endowed with the gift of being able to enjoy the many shades of grey that exist between no orgasm and *an* orgasm. For it is a gift – not an insufficiency. If this fact were acknowledged proudly, it would be a significant and genuine move toward true 'empowerment', i.e. self-knowledge. While women should obviously appreciate that they, unlike men, can have *multiple* orgasms, and more intense ones at that, they should also take pride in the fact that, unlike men, they can still derive a great deal of pleasure *without* 'achieving' an orgasm at all. Despite the Health Education Authority's asinine talk of male orgasms not being 'essential', or how men should be more restrained, taking time to learn about the more subtle and intimate pleasures to be experienced through general foreplay – come, they must – and a failure to do this is nothing short of a ghastly tragedy with dire physical and emotional consequences. While of course men savour the journey, such a voyage must have a final destination. To do otherwise is comparable to a starving man being allowed to eat food without being able to swallow it. There is no penultimate for men and no sexual consolation prize if they forego their orgasms.

Sexual enlightenment is full of contradictions. One of its more unfortunate consequences has been to make people too conscious of the process, which inadvertently detracts from the human experience. 'Thinking', 'considering', 'deliberating', 'choosing', 'planning' are wonderful concepts when applied to one's business plan, but have little place in passion, romance and sex. This of course pleases a wide variety of vested interests, ranging from the Department of Health to the Terrence Higgins Trust. We have witnessed the emergence of a managed sexuality: a lot of thought has gone into it, but what has been compromised is the *feeling*.

7: A Toast to Low Self-esteem

While the term 'self-esteem' first appeared in the *Manchester Examiner* in 1884, it would be nearly a century before it would reach prominence in popular and professional literature. It was the 'black is beautiful' movement and the women's movement of the 1970s in the United States which hurled this concept into public eminence. Between 1979 and 1985 alone, more than 1,416 articles, 30 psychometric tests and measures, and over 50 manuscripts were published on the subject of self-esteem. Most of this was associated with the effort to raise the general feeling of self-worth amongst the children of ethnic minority groups who were thought to experience discrimination and bias. When the women's movement decided to define women as a minority group whose self-esteem had suffered in a similar way to that of ethnic minorities, the focus of attention was widened to include them. However, instead of attributing their lack of self-esteem solely to white men, they generously expanded their definition of culpability, allowing *all* men to share the blame. All of this culminated with the release of the LP by John Lennon, with a song by his wife, Yoko Ono, entitled *Woman is the Nigger of the World*.

The 1990s have seen a growing concern about society's collective self-esteem, which has reached state government level. California, for example, established the California Task Force to Promote Self-Esteem and Personal and Social Responsibility. After three years of research, the Task Force concluded that self-esteem and its corollary, personal responsibility, are key components of a healthy society, which have been warped and undersupported by the criminal justice, education and social systems. Their final report included dozens of recommendations for legislators, educators and individuals on how to promote self-esteem as a form of 'social medicine'. Some of their suggestions were: combating teenage gangs with self-esteem programmes in schools, and training staff members who work with those on social security to teach self-esteem. The report concluded: 'When we build our lives around an accurate and appropriate appreciation of our own worth as human beings, persons who are capable of dealing with life and worthy of dignity and respect just because we are human, then we are most productive, most caring and responsible in our relationships with others and most fulfilled within ourselves.' Legislation on self-esteem was last seen moving through the California legislature. Other states have followed suit with state-financed task forces based on California's model for the research and promotion of self-esteem.

In the United States the Institute for the Advancement of Health held a conference which addressed the issue of 'emotional literacy', which was defined as 'competence in the area of emotional, social, and behavioural skills and is achieved through "affective learning" or "emotional learning".' Affective learning was thought to develop self-awareness and self-esteem and should therefore be introduced into the school curriculum. One of the key speakers explained that: 'Children in our school systems are rewarded for accumulating information but not for developing self-esteem or life-affirming values.' Encouraging children from a young age to understand an emotional world and inviting them to communicate within it, is one of the few suggestions for mass psychology that seems feasible because it is intended to be *preventative*, intervening at a stage of development during which some influence can be exerted. This is a stark departure from the adult versions of rapid self-esteem enhancement, which attempt to be curative.

More than any other, the concept of self-esteem has now

been used to explain most areas of human success and failure, from compulsive eating to job promotion to the quality of one's relationships. Self-esteem has even been linked to the likelihood of developing coronary heart disease. It has been thought for several years that aggressive 'Type-A' personalities – specifically the most hostile and suspicious of such ambitious achievement-orientated individuals – are at greater risk of heart disease than their more relaxed 'Type-B' counterparts. More recently, it has been suggested that those 'Type-A' individuals with low self-esteem are at greater risk than those with higher self-esteem. The mechanism that protects the individual with high self-esteem is thought to consist of a superior ability to cope with stress. A belief in oneself, self-esteem, may enable a person to treat challenges with less trepidation, which in turn is translated into a healthier nervous system response.

Self-esteem is considered the bottom line of one's fortitude, the key aspect of the 'self' upon which everything else depends. While some factors, such as genetics, up-bringing, physical appearance, are seen as playing a central role in determining one's self-esteem, there are other factors such as weight, career and relationships, which can operate in either direction. A degree in psychology is quite unnecessary to be aware that losing weight, getting promoted at work, or starting a new relationship can raise self-esteem immediately, while gaining weight, getting fired, or being dumped can go some way toward lowering self-esteem.

While it has been most illuminating to hear of the various factors which contribute to or detract from self-esteem, the most lucrative area at the moment for psychology is *raising* self-esteem. For if everything about oneself is dependent on self-esteem, raising the level of one's self-esteem should result in a wide range of life improvements. Improving one's self-esteem is *the* supreme form of self-improvement. There is of course no question that various courses of action can have short-term effects on one's perceived sense of self-worth: but it remains to be seen whether people *really* make lasting changes to their underlying level of self-esteem. Moreover, is there really a unitary global form of self-esteem, or do people have different levels of more specific types of self-esteem associated with all the different areas of their life? Such questions are not subject to Newtonian laws. Despite this, however, society has been exposed to a deluge of proclamations which deal with these issues, through a plethora of books, courses and therapies all purporting to understand the mechanisms and dynamics of self-esteem and providing answers and solutions. Such a trend has been accompanied by phrases like 'you must learn to love yourself or nobody else will.' This is reinforced by the fact that in Britain in particular we only see the public side of most people, particularly those influential people we admire. Those 'who love themselves' go places, do things, have things, feel things and taste things that are inaccessible to those who don't, in the way that the weight-loss industry promotes the idea that slimness also brings about these benefits. The new imperative to love yourself brings with it its own form of disappointment and oppression, for it demands that one goes beyond merely knowing and acknowledging oneself, which is in itself often quite a lifetime's achievement. Feeling bad about not feeling good about oneself, contributes little toward one's self-esteem.

In Britain, it is generally believed that self-esteem is also related to social class: upper-class individuals possessing a greater sense of 'self-worth' than working-class individuals. Many also believe that the boarding school experience is the most 'character build-ing' and 'produces' individuals with greater 'self-confidence' – individuals who wake up each morning and feel a sense both of their ability and their entitlement. Few, except possibly those who have actually attended boarding schools themselves, seem to question this assumption. Many seem to confuse the observation that boarding school education is linked with the greater opportunity to attain and achieve things, with the idea that a boarding school education actually confers upon the individual greater self-esteem in the fullest sense of the word. In doing this, one is saying that parents play a less important role in child-rearing. Such responsibilities, it is thought, should be delegated to those that are more expert. If this were true, however, why is it that privileged people in other Western cultures do not, as a rule, send their children off to boarding school to develop a higher sense of self-esteem? Boarding school education certainly provides a far greater *intensity* of education facilitated by a controlled environment. This in itself places the individual in a highly advantageous position when it comes time to consider university or profession. Moreover, boarding school will later provide enormous social advantages by preventing the social contamination secretly feared by the 'comfortable classes' that occurs when one's child is exposed to the lower orders: everything from accent, the gait and cadence of one's walk, the habit of spitting in public, to parents who read little else but one another's tattoos. Educated parents are aware, at least subconsciously, that children are easily seduced by the garish facade of 'yoof' culture which, in the short-term, is inherently more attractive and appealing than some of the more subtle and enduring interests of the educated classes. Like the naive local natives of Third World countries who were taken in by merchants who offered cheap, brightly coloured plastic goods and baseball caps in exchange for rarer and more valuable goods, children are impressionable and their values and interests are formed early. The joke: Q: 'What do you call the box attached to the back of a satellite dish?' A: 'A Council house,' does not occur without good reason.

It is, however, most amusing to watch the guilt-ridden, liberal intelligentsia parents explain their 'difficult decision' to send Julian to public school. The reason invariably proffered is that it is the 'poor teaching' that they're trying to avoid – 'he'll receive a better education' – though no mention is made of the 'additional' form of 'education' Julian would otherwise be receiving at his local state school, which may include extra tuition in *Untermenschen* etiquette as mentioned above, along with additional tuition in 'creative writing', otherwise referred to as 'graffiti', and a liberal dose of 'Estuary English elocution' thrown in, all at no extra charge. If Julian were to attend the local state comprehensive he would, in order to survive, have to adapt by becoming a social chameleon, adopting many of the 'salt-of-the-earth' interests of his fellow pupils. Parents who, at the birth of their child, express the wish for their child to grow up being part of the 'whole community', start back-pedalling furiously when little Julian reaches school age and there is a choice between the state nursery and the nice little Montessori around the corner. No doubt such 'caring' parents are well aware that no amount of self-improvement courses or self-help books will later overcome the influence of this choice on Julian's formative years.

Self-esteem cannot be bought, and while it is true that the 'product' of a top boarding school may display the veneer of self-esteem – the ability to put themselves or their ideas forward without any apparent self-doubt – what goes on at a deeper, more subtle level is often difficult to assess. The effects may take many years to manifest themselves, showing up later within personal relationships, marriage and sexual behaviour, and ultimately being reflected in one's own ability to parent. As such intimate areas are somewhat elusive to outside investigation, society is left to focus upon the more tangible outcomes that boarding school is thought to influence. Ludovic Kennedy revealed a most poignant childhood memory when he said that his parents brought him up to believe that they loved him . . . but then, at the age of 7, they sent him off to boarding school.

What seems to escape the attention of many such traditional parents is the fact that children need continuous amounts of unconditional love, preferably from their biological parents. Moreover, they need unconditional love when *they* need it – not at predetermined times such as school holidays or weekends – and they need it in person, not in writing or over the telephone. Despite the claims of smiling public school headmasters and mistresses that their school is 'just one big happy family', 'happy families' exist in an environment of unconditional love, while love in boarding school is *conditional*. Amongst boys in particular, such 'boarding school love' is not conferred lightly, in fact it is often 'performance-related' whereby, for example, achievement on the rugger field is rewarded with the love of one's peers.

There are additional problems with the fallacy of boarding school love. If children are disciplined at school and later complain to their parents that they feel the treatment was somehow unjustified or unfair, they may well find that their rather diplomatic, tactful parents compound their hurt by trivialising their child's complaint with the logic 'well darling, it happened over three weeks ago, put it behind you now' or even 'well if they punished you, then you probably deserved it.' Whether it is justified or not, the parents' response is interpreted by the child as an abdication of their parental responsibility in favour of school authorities: emotional betrayal and treachery on the most grand scale imaginable. Boarding schools also have their relative pecking orders and while winners may benefit immensely, later to emerge brimming with confidence – those who are less competitive, more sensitive, or unsporty, can, in relative terms, be on the bottom rung, much worse for one's self-esteem than being on the top rung at a state school. However, those on the outside don't hear of these cases –

they're too enamoured of society's boarding school success stories.

Britain is not a nation destined to invent terms such as 'Go For It!' – a slogan which presupposes a sufficient degree of God-given self-esteem. This does not seem to be the case in the United States, where people are known as 'citizens' as opposed to 'subjects' and there is the veneer of true equality, a democracy with tokens such as a written constitution. The problem with this arrangement is that, unlike Britain, where ordinary people who are perfectly competent at what they do feel somehow unworthy and therefore unable to put their view forward confidently and assertively, one finds in America, every Tom, Dick and Harry labouring under the misapprehension that his ideas are wonderful and that he has a right to be President even if he's a complete and utter fool. In any event, he knows his 'rights'. International journalists who find themselves having to interview members of the general public consistently observe the fact that, as Ian Peacock, an experienced reporter for BBC World Service and Radio 4, points out:

British people have a much more 'us and them' attitude to the media and don't seem to feel worthy of interest from the media. The British see the media as the aristocracy, or at least part of the establishment – a techno-castle – and don't feel they have any real access to it. They view themselves as 'subjects' to the media – as privileged to have been chosen. They ask with predictable regularity: 'Are you *really* from the BBC?' Americans are not afraid of their intellect nor of expressing it, whereas the British see the public expression of intellect as pretentious, so they become jocular, self-ridiculing, 'why would you want to hear what I have to think?' And in the case of a couple, the woman will immediately seal her lips, step back, point to and direct all enquiries to her partner.

Highly competent professional women with good ideas often lament the fact that they 'don't have the confidence' to advance their ideas and desires in a direct and assertive way. The fact that they can comment objectively indicates that they are well aware of the gap between the way they do behave, think and feel, and the way they would like to behave, think and feel. They are led to believe that there is something wrong with them that needs to be rectified. Men are often used as the yardstick of self-confidence by which to judge oneself, but as was mentioned in Chapter 4, it is easy to confuse an aggressive drive with self-confidence. Moreover, as is often pointed out, most of the world's 'power houses' are run on a male value system which favours male forms of assertiveness and apparent self-confidence. As a result, many see the solution as being quite obvious: adopt the appropriate values and behaviours that will get you where you want to go; male values and male behaviours. If one hadn't noticed already, the world of men is extremely 'goal orientated' with relatively linear paths which lead to clearly defined objectives. It also helps to be naturally endowed with qualities of single-mindedness and the divine right of selfishness, with a fifteen-fold advantage of testosterone to fuel one's ascendancy.

One of the solutions is to acquire the outward manifestations of self-esteem through methods such as 'Assertiveness Training'. The Great British public were afforded the opportunity to 'Assert Yourself' with the Channel 4 series and booklet of that name, which informed them that: 'Over the past few years, many people have learned another way of behaving . . . the assertive way.' After explaining that 'Lack of self-confidence is frequently the reason for people's inappropriate or bizarre behaviour,' they offer a route to recovery. 'In the past 40 to 50 years, behavioural scientists and psychologists have formulated the view that just as we *learn* the way we behave and react to different situations, so we can "unlearn" such behaviour. These theories provide the basis for assertiveness training; put simply, you can learn to *change* ("change" being the operative word).' Such brazen assumptions exemplify the worst aspects of psychology and how it has been elevated to a form of received wisdom within mainstream thinking. Contained within this attempt at mass-market self-improvement are all the key words: 'learn', 'unlearn' and 'change', and the predictable faulty logic which states that by knowing how something works, you can of course go on to change it. However, we are not toasters.

Moreover, acquiring 'Assertiveness Techniques' through 'The Assertive Way' fails to take into account that 'behaviours', 'techniques', and 'ways' are the end product of self-esteem and just as forcing yourself to smile when you are feeling suicidal does not make you optimistic, so mimicking the perceived trappings of high self-esteem does not necessarily confer self-confidence upon one. It is most interesting to note that in the section entitled 'Rights to Assertiveness', while one is told: 'that as human beings, we have certain rights: . . . the right to state our needs . . . to say "yes" or "no" to other people's demands . . . the right to be treated as an intelligent, capable and equal human being . . . the right to make mistakes . . . the right to change your mind . . . the right to ask for what you want . . . the right to express your own opinions and values . . . the right to express your feelings', there is no mention of the right to be shy, sensitive or unassertive. This is a consistent oversight amongst those involved in empowering the individual, for some people are by nature shy, sensitive and unassertive and if anything, great effort should instead be put into helping them feel justified in being this way.

T-shirts often have a way of clarifying issues and one in particular reads: So you want me to be assertive? Well I *Won't*!

What is perceived as a lack of confidence for women in the work place is partly a lack of ability to adopt behaviours and values which are not second nature. At the same time, tools such as 'feminine wiles' have been discouraged as being underhanded and manipulative, while sleeping one's way to the top is nowadays considered despicable, and though men may not disapprove of this in principle, they are in fact becoming increasingly concerned at being left open to accusations of sexual harassment. So by putting their traditional aptitudes aside, ironically, women have been forced into a very difficult position.

The UK medical journal, *The Lancet*, published an article entitled 'Self-Esteem':

The notion of self-esteem arises because we tend to estimate the value of other individuals and ourselves. People may have a good, middling or bad opinion of themselves – rather surprisingly, these are global evaluations. We may indeed have opinions of our capacity at cricket, and at maths, and at doing the cha-cha, but we also have a global opinion of our general worth. Another surprising thing about self-esteem is the enormous range of variation between individuals, which is immeasurably greater than the range of variation that a single individual undergoes from time to time. Some people think the whole world is their oyster; others feel they have no right to exist.

Our global opinion of our general self-worth is thought to be determined by a number of things ranging from genetics to up-bringing, to things which, on the surface, seem transient, such as acne. Self-esteem is, however, not a constant in any given individual and can vary on a day-to-day basis and can even fluctuate within minutes of hearing bad news or good news. Factors ranging from one's menstrual cycle to the amount of sleep one is, or is not, getting, to one's eating patterns and blood sugar levels, to the time of year and the amount of daylight one is getting, to whether or not one has had the living daylights fucked out of them the night before, to the number of media images of beautiful, slim, young, happy models to which one is exposed (the male counterpart being tall men with muscles, a full head of hair, a swollen wallet, and an ego-mobile with a buxom bombshell in the passenger seat), should all be taken into account.

Michael Waller has proposed a fascinating theory, first published in *Nature*. In essence he sees one's level of self-esteem as one of the factors playing a part in finding a partner and having children – 'psycho-Darwinism'. While it is normally thought that we look for attractive characteristics in a prospective partner and that we may reject them if their characteristics are not up to standard, Michael Waller has turned this idea on its head by suggesting that we also look for attractive characteristics in *ourselves* before giving permission to ourselves to procreate. In other words, low self-esteem results in our brains deciding that we are not genetically worthy enough to reproduce. It is interesting to note that low self-esteem is associated with a lowered libido. It is suggested that there are 'comparator' genes which impel those who carry them to routinely assess themselves in terms of their relative performance within a peer group, or on the basis of their valuation by their parents. High self-assessment will engender a sense of emotional well-being, while low self-assessment will result in conditions such as depression, chronic anxiety, self-destructive behaviour and impotence. This fits in rather nicely with the social comparison theory of psychology which acknowledges our proclivity to constantly assess ourselves in relation to others.

While it is hard to believe that we are altruistic to the extent of foregoing the opportunity to reproduce, or to at least have a good fuck, there is a method in the apparent madness. In addition to low self-esteem being associated with lowered libido, it is, as *The Lancet* suggests: 'interesting to medicine because low self-esteem is associated with diseases such as depressive illness, anxiety states and psychosomatic disorders . . . if a depressive state is triggered, a further fall in self-esteem is part of the depressive process.' Suicide, drug abuse and alcohol abuse and serious eating disorders tend to reduce one's ability to reproduce as well as one's chances of being considered desirable by the opposite sex, and even by oneself, thereby further lowering one's chances of reproducing by withdrawing from the gene pool. But what is the benefit of bowing out of the sexual scenario in a genetic sense?

Michael Waller believes that although, as a race, we differ in many genetic characteristics, there are some core genes that we all share as a species which are a prerequisite to survival; for example, those that cause cells to replicate or hearts to form. These are also referred to as 'ancient genes'. And so at a very primitive, genetic level, we are part of a much larger family than we normally think. In short, by allowing *your* version of these vital genes to be contaminated with other characteristics, such as extreme feelings of worthlessness and depression, which are 'weak', you are leaving the next generation vulnerable because of the poor packaging of these vital genes. It is preferable for such core genes to be accompanied by an organism which feels as happy and worthy as possible, thus ensuring that your core genes are passed on by others more able to ensure their continuing survival. A bit like a rugby match whereby a chap carrying the ball realises that he is vulnerable and about to be brought to the ground, so he passes the ball back to another member who he knows has a better chance of scoring a try and ensuring team victory. This is even reflected in the field of education where an apparent Catch 22 situation seems to exist for those with very low self-esteem. Educational psychologists have found that while putting forth the effort to learn more on one's own should improve a sense of self-worth, one's self-esteem must already be high or the effort will not seem worthwhile. In such cases, the awful genetic home-truth is: 'don't learn to love yourself, you're just not worth it.'

This is not to say that people do not inherit a predisposition toward low self-esteem or unhappiness. The idea that our personalities, our moods and our character are not influenced by what came before would seem highly counter-intuitive. It seems that the way these predispositions interact with what occurs during the formative years after birth will ultimately determine one's global sense of self-worth: one's self-esteem. Predictably, the interaction that goes on between baby and parent is where it all starts.

Ideally, in the most mutual form of interplay, the mother's or father's responses should mirror their child's emotions and expressions. This is thought to help the child value himself or herself highly but accurately, the child having an accurate 'feed-back' system on tap with judges he or she can trust. However, problems begin to develop when a child is ignored, perhaps, for example, because of the parents' continual pre-occupation with other things, or depression. Further corruption can occur when the parent insists that the child mirrors his or her emotions and aspirations. The distorted feedback that results can greatly exaggerate blame or praise, with the child knowing instinctively that these have more to do with the parent's needs than with the child's true value. However, in order to retain the parent's love and approval, the child begins to relinquish his or her own accurate self-perception. The over-valuation, under-valuation and distortion of the child's identity result in inaccurate and troublesome self-judgement: one is never quite satisfied and must continually do more or do better. The self-improvement industry takes over where the parents left off, helping people to question their own versions of themselves, encouraging people to aspire to other ways of feeling and behaving, thereby adding to the distortion of one's already troubled identity.

Girls in particular are encouraged to play down their own abilities or to attribute their hard won achievements to serendipity. This of course goes down particularly well in Britain where self-abasement is a valued national characteristic anyway. Women also retain and mull over negative information while selectively ignoring much of the positive. For most women self-esteem is precariously subject to other people's opinions and for some, it is often impossible to accept or even hear a compliment: 'I just don't know how to take a compliment. In fact, I'd much rather have a playful insult, then I can at least hit back.' This later manifests itself in women judging other women much more harshly than they do men. They also appraise themselves and other women less favourably than they do men for the same work, and expect women to work harder and longer in order to be worthy of the same rewards. The 'Queen Bee' syndrome.

Male culture on the surface appears to encourage very much the reverse. Self-promotion and even outright bragging are commendable qualities and one can never receive too many compliments. From the outside, men appear to ignore much of the negative, even when they should take note of it; this may be due in part to their lesser ability to 'read' people, retaining and basking in the glory of success and accomplishments which they have no doubt justly deserved. As is the case in many aspects of the British class system, such self-promotion is viewed quite differently amongst the upper classes where, again, something close to an inversion of values prevails. Any success must appear effortless and demands an air of assumed nonchalance to maintain a distance from those aspiring, purposeful, middle-class professionals so preoccupied with their busy 'careers'. This is reflected in the division between Arts versus Sciences and the association of the upper classes with the Arts at the expense of the Sciences which are considered too earthly and purposeful, the logic being that it is those who must concern themselves with earning a living that must familiarise themselves with practical skills. The scientist is seen as almost an up-market version of a tradesman: he who must concern himself with function as opposed to beauty. In fact, many an elitist can be heard feigning scientific ignorance, almost to the point of hamming it up, in an attempt to make clear the fact that they are 'cultured' in the true sense of the word. 'Gosh! low density lipoprotein cholesterol, how interesting, do tell me about it!'

Class aside, unfavourable physical characteristics that become prominent during one's formative years can be devastating to one's self-esteem in the long run. Recently acne has become acknowledged as such an affliction. While at one time adolescents were routinely told 'don't worry, you'll grow out of it' and 'other people won't notice it half as much as you', there is evidence that the emotional scars can last forever. Acne is not merely a skin complaint: one's face is one's identity and as an adolescent, if one's face is scarred and undesirable, so is one's identity. It is interesting to observe women, many of whom escaped acne during their teenage years only to find that the hormone changes that occur in their late twenties bring on mild acne at this unexpected stage. They certainly don't like it. What is perceived as a superficial skin complaint can ultimately affect self-esteem in as serious a way as childhood abuse. However, because it involves no-one else and doesn't make good headlines which conjure up images of sex or beatings, it is treated far more lightly.

While it can be useful to gain an understanding of the various factors which ultimately contribute to our general sense of self-esteem, this does not, as some would have us believe, confer upon one the ability to make profound changes to one's level of self-esteem. We are still not toasters. This is not necessarily, however, a reason to despair, for though it may not be fashionable, it is highly possible to lead and enjoy a life with low self-esteem. Many do it already without even thinking about it in those terms.

What the prevailing psychological climate will not allow us to accept is the fact that in many ways the die is cast and windows of opportunity have been missed. This is part of what forms our identity; moreover, it is a part of life to which psychology is diametrically opposed. This is not to say that we should try to lead a life which lowers our self-esteem further by associating with people or activities which 'make us feel bad about ourselves'. By avoiding the exacerbation of low self-esteem, while at the same time trying to associate with people and activities which 'make us feel good about ourselves', life can certainly be made easier. However, what psychology doesn't make clear, is that this is not the same as making a profound change in one's basic level of self-esteem. It is often life itself which achieves this inadvertently: self-esteem can be raised unexpectedly through life events, such as becoming a parent or grand-parent – a positive view of genetics – and even through death events, as seen in the case of 'merry widows'.

8: A Weight off My Mind

Conceptions of 'the self' embrace the psychological and physical, which in the world of self-worth are inextricably linked, the dividing line between embarking upon emotional changes as opposed to physical changes being nowadays almost non-existent. For many, the quickest route to alleviating a state of unhappiness is to avoid therapy and go on a diet immediately. However, contemporary psychology has invited itself into an arena in which it doesn't belong. Most people have by now been inculcated with the idea that being overweight is as much the result of psychological factors as physical and biological ones. Expressions such as 'comfort eating' are now accepted as received wisdom, courtesy of contemporary psychology which enjoys reading as much as possible into the reasons why people eat. Many of the ideas which originate in the psychological literature are successfully misappropriated by various authors and factions within the diet industry, who present such theories as facts which can be applied to fat – 'weight management'.

Psychology is most noticeable when one is searching for the 'reasons' as to why one is overweight, and there is a varied menu to choose from. You are no doubt overweight because: you are unhappy; you are unfulfilled; you are bored; your boyfriend has impregnated your sister, or your husband is a homosexual and your hamster just died; you feel trapped; you've never had an orgasm; you've had a row; you're feeling guilty – but don't know why; you're boiling with rage; there's a romantic weepy on TV; you've had an affair; you've just seen someone who is prettier and slimmer than you; and so on. The convenient aspect of 'psychologising' weight is that the interpretations can be never-ending, with a new in-depth explanation waiting just around the corner. Typically, the authors of such books will first ingratiate themselves with the reader through the use of empathy: 'I know, I've been there.' Various emotional themes will be related, leading the reader to further believe that it is their emotional state that is responsible for their weight 'problem'. It would of course be too obvious (and concise) to point out the fact that maybe anyone who feels overweight in our society is likely to feel unhappy. It is not a mere coincidence that it is more lucrative to convince women to believe they are overweight because they are unhappy, as opposed to being unhappy because they believe they are overweight.

Let us, for example, examine the phenomenon of 'comfort eating'. The term itself implies that one is insecure and that food is used as a psychological mechanism to achieve a form of comfort. However, other less interesting explanations for seemingly unnecessary eating are not entertained. Menstrual cycles, for example, can have a huge impact on eating, but are considered rather dull and messy. During the second half of a woman's menstrual cycle, *the luteal phase*, profound changes in hormones begin to occur, resulting in many cases in a significant lowering of blood sugar levels. When this happens, in both men and women, they become hungry and irritable and more prone to aggression, which in primitive times would ensure that humans killed for food. Nowadays, women still become irritable, but they can satisfy their biologically based hunger with a never-ending variety of food choices. For many women, pre-menstrual syndrome (PMS) can occur for a full two weeks every month, beginning the day after ovulation, with the symptoms including wild fluctuations in blood sugar levels, growing ever worse as they approach the start of their periods. What this means in practical terms is that for 26 weeks of the year, their appetites are less controllable than usual and their emotions may swing dramatically. Contemporary psychology would, of course, prefer to attribute the change in appetite to the emotional rather than the physical changes because it is obviously much more interesting and saleable to interpret it this way. In fact, the idea of chocolate causing spots is the product of such reversed logic. Women are more likely to eat chocolate during the second half of their menstrual cycle, a time when they are also more likely to develop spots because of the changes in their hormones. Naturally, to satisfy the female need to feel guilty for eating chocolate, society would prefer to see spots as the product of such Epicurean indulgences. In fact, studies which required subjects to eat vast amounts of chocolate have failed repeatedly to find any relationship between chocolate intake and spots.

It is worth pursuing our understanding of the reasons for PMS, something which nobody seems to take time to think about. PMS was, until recently, dismissed by many doctors as being 'purely psychological'. When the feminist movement was at its most vocal, women were encouraged to deny the existence of PMS for fear of assisting their 'male oppressors' in portraying them as the less capable, less stable gender. Even now, there are feminist academics who persist in claiming their studies show PMS as a culturally invented phenomenon with little evidence to support it. However, women aren't as stupid as feminists may think. Some scientists believe that PMS was at one time vital for the survival of the human race. In primitive times, life was somewhat precarious and uncomfortable and short. Food supplies were scarce and it was beneficial for men to hunt in groups at the same time. However, in order to ensure that men would have nothing better to do, women evolved the ability to synchronise their menstrual cycles. The fortunate (or unfortunate) consequence of this was that for a certain specified period of time each month, women would not be very nice to be around and, because of their lower blood sugar levels, would make more demands for food. What better time to go off on a hunting expedition with one's friends to return later to a good meal and some serious fertilising. Moreover, women had far fewer periods in this era, for they were pregnant a great deal of the time and died at a very young age. Studies of female baboons have found that they never menstruated in the wild because they were always pregnant and it was only when they entered captivity that menstruation started. Therefore some scientists view both menstruation and PMS as being very much modern phenomena and unnatural in evolutionary terms.

In modern society, these primitive tendencies have been greatly exaggerated, for example, stress and even caffeine cause further fluctuations in blood sugar levels and, combined with enormous changes in lifestyle, have resulted in everyone having the opportunity to eat as much as they want. One couldn't purposely engineer a better plan to fatten up the Western world: transportation, labour-saving devices, sedentary lifestyles, a staggering international variety of food choices which can be stored and cooked in any number of ways, major food corporations which add large amounts of fat to their products, television programmes, radio programmes, magazines, books and advertisements about food, not to mention the age of the 'dial-a-pizza'. According to the American Agriculture Department, the food industry spends $36 billion a year on advertising in the United States, while the Federal Government hands each state $50,000 for nutritional education in schools. Despite a growing awareness of the link between nutrition and health, and despite the continued growth of the diet industry – now estimated to have revenues of between $40 billion and $50 billion a year – Americans, and children in particular, are growing more obese than ever before.

In Britain, the snack-food market alone is worth more than

£3 billion a year in sales and is one of the fastest-growing areas of food retailing. Billions more are spent by consumers on fast food and other high-fat products. In fact, the food industry has been so successful at selling such food that more than half of men and more than a third of women are overweight or obese, according to the Department of Health. This is a considerable increase on the past decade, with no end in sight. It is actually in the interests of certain sections of the Government that the public grows larger. Curiously, the Ministry of Agriculture looks after the interests of both the food industry and the public, a slight conflict of loyalties to say the least. In fact, they recently attempted to prevent the Committee on Medical Aspects of Food Policy (known ironically as COMA), from publishing their recommendations in a form that would be comprehensible to the public. In addition, the snack and food industry, led by giant firms such as United Biscuits, Mars, Cadbury Schweppes and Tate & Lyle, tried to stop the Department of Health from recommending to the public a 50 per cent reduction in their consumption of cakes, biscuits and soft drinks, and a 20 per cent reduction in sugar and jam.

To suggest that those who are overweight should look deeply into their souls for the 'underlying reasons' is ridiculous to say the least, but can be terribly profitable. The cakes are stacked against you.

Returning to 'comfort eating', food is also one of the many forms of recreation and stimulation as well as being a way of killing time. There is no psychology behind this. In the way that one turns on the television, picks up a book, rings a friend, fiddles with a pen or smokes a cigarette, food is something to do, as opposed to staring at the wall or sleeping; however, because activities involving books or telephone conversations do not possess calories, there is little point in subjecting them to psychological scrutiny. If people are, for example, 'unfulfilled', by definition they probably have less stimulation on a minute to minute basis and may therefore be able to fill their time through the forms of recreation mentioned above. However, if they suddenly find themselves in an exciting and stimulating job they are likely to be rather preoccupied, with less opportunity or capacity to handle any extra stimulation, e.g. food. But again, it is far more interesting to explain this in emotional terms.

Psychology, in addition to inviting itself in to explain why you are overweight, offers psychological techniques to help you change the way and the amount you eat. This is rather cruel considering that those behind such advice are well aware of the overbearing influences which compel society to eat and eat. And eat. This area of self-improvement in particular can be most self-destructive, for there is nothing like low esteem to make one reach for a diet and there is nothing like failing to stick to a diet to make one feel even lower. Even the more recent move away from 'diets' as we know them, still involves 'thinking' about food and 'what it means to you'. Again, the responsibility for one's weight is shifted to the self and there is no collective responsibility for the blame. Implicit in this view is the judgement that society's obesity is, to a large extent, due to gluttony and sloth. While at one time fat was solely a nutritional issue, it then became a Feminist Issue and more recently a psychology issue.

When challenged about their aspiration to slimness and the inevitable dieting which ensues, it has been fashionable for women to claim: 'I'm doing it for *me*.' One finds the same response when the discussion turns to make-up, hair, clothing and even underwear. It is also acceptable to say 'I do it for other women.' One further variation on this logic reads 'If I look good, I feel more empowered and people therefore respond to me accordingly.' Other people's responses to one's appearance seem almost incidental in this version of events – the *consequence* of one's appearance, certainly not the main driving force behind one's makeover. There was a time when women could be more honest and concede that such aesthetic endeavours were, to a large extent, intended to make them more attractive to men. Both ancient and 'primitive' cultures find women as well as men accentuating their attractive features in a way which appeals to and gains an advantage with the opposite sex. Some of the first signs of human artistry are carved body ornaments, and findings of worn pieces of ochre indicate that primitive man may have applied the red and black chalklike substance as make-up. In the current climate, however, preening is conceptualised as a facet of empowerment for oneself and any such public proclamations to the contrary could be seen as rendering oneself servile to a value system which is unfair. Curiously, when asked to choose their one creature comfort, women who appear as guests on *Desert Island Discs* seem to forget to mention 'a bathroom scale' or 'a mirror'.

There is no point in denying the fact that we must all operate within a 'sexual economy' in order to find and retain a partner. There are strong parallels with that other, more generally recognised economy, better known for its stock exchange and pink newspaper. While this metaphor may at first appear rather crass – a market place of human behaviour with infinite variables of trading activity – most of us accept this aspect of life, albeit unknowingly. Those who feel that this view is demeaning to humans, likening us to a market in cattle, goats or donkeys, are ignoring the relative sophistication of such markets. By dint of making endless comparisons, we form detailed judgements on the relative competitiveness of our stock-in-trade, i.e. ourselves. Moreover, many people agonise constantly as to the worth of their 'assets', both physical and cerebral. The benefits of possessing general physical attractiveness are to be found in many areas of life. Research has found that attractive people are *assumed* to have other desirable characteristics as well, routinely judged to be, among other things, more intelligent, to have happier marriages, to be more successful in their careers and social lives. Studies have found that the same piece of work, for example a college essay, will be evaluated more favourably when a physically attractive person is thought to have produced it.

Looks are also *the* most important factor for men, when choosing women. However, women consistently misjudge what they believe looks 'ideal' to men. It may assist those consumed by dissatisfaction with their appearance to at least learn to hate the *right* aspects of themselves. Women wrongly view weight as being *the* major factor which determines a woman's sexual self-worth − her 'market placing'. This subversion of women's ability to judge accurately who men prefer to fuck and have relationships with, is the result of some recent changes in the reference points available for assessing oneself. The advent of the mirror enabled people to scrutinise their attributes in a way and with a frequency not possible before. This brought with it problems of its own, but combined with the new omnipresent point of comparison, the fashion model, things went terribly awry. Pat Kane has expressed deep concern over the implications of the 'new' photography:

> We believe the camera's eye can bring us truth, whether subjective (the snapshot of the loved one, the film performance of a great actor) or objective (pictures of weather forecasts, police suspects, lab experiments). The photograph is the way we moderns test that reality is actually *out there*: we rely on its veracity far more than we readily admit. But even at the very inception of photography, fears that it could produce illusion were often expressed − and justified. Louis Jacques Daguerre, the co-patenter of the photographic process, was also a notorious illusionist: he began experimenting with

his 'pencil of nature' almost immediately, shading tones and retouching details.

The advent of digital imaging has irreversibly changed any concept of photographic realism. Filmed or videoed images are converted to *pixels*, which can be manipulated by computer to any form, in order to suit any requirements – specifically, the requirements of the beauty, fashion and advertising industries. What this means in practical terms is that, when viewing the photograph of a model, the picture editor can, and does, make a wide variety of staggering digital alterations to the image: changing the eye colour, enlarging the pupils, whitening the eyes, carving away the hips, lengthening the legs, erasing any blemishes or wrinkles etc., all carried out in the comfort of one's office whilst sitting in front of a VDU screen. As Kane observes, 'In the strangest of paradoxes, digital imaging is turning the photographic *back into a form of painting*, with a slight whiff of the magical and occult about it . . . reality is an infinitely mixable palette.'

The saga continues, for there are questions as to who influences the choice and promotion of a certain body shape. The big fashion designers tend to be gay men and this is bound to influence the fashion world's definition of what constitutes an attractive figure – a narrow, boyish shape – which is in turn reflected in the clothes that are designed and the models that are chosen to promote such designs. And the saga continues. What is most insidious is the creation of a fraudulent association between slender figures and remarkably beautiful faces in all forms of visual media, while in reality, a slim figure confers no greater likelihood of possessing a pretty face. The fact that one never seems to find a slim model with the facial appeal of a pit bull terrier remains a rather puzzling matter. The result of this has been a corruption of what is both within the realms of normality and what is believed to be desirable to men. Waif-like models with household names are sick role models for women – not sex symbols for men, who would far rather fuck, marry and have children with much fuller versions. Men generally want to fuck, marry and have children with women whose hips, thighs and bottoms are markedly different from their own: it is called 'otherness'.

Men value curvaceous female figures. Studies have supported the obvious, that people consistently judge a woman's figure not by whether she is slim or fat, but by the *ratio* of her waist to her hips. The ideal proportion – the hips being approximately a third greater than the waist – reflects a hormone profile that results in women being more likely to store fat on their hips as opposed to their waists – the 'pear shape' – a form which is strongly associated with higher fertility and resistance to disease. The Western world's recent obsession with slenderness has not altered this equation. For example, while over the past several decades the winner of the Miss America contest has become 30 per cent thinner, the ratio of her waist to her hips has remained close to this ancient template. Further studies consistently find a significant disparity between the female body shape that women *think* men generally prefer, and the female body shape men actually do prefer. One can imagine which gender chose the more slender example.

To convince pear-shaped sceptics of the validity of these sexual observations, it will be necessary to return to the ultimate testing ground for the economic theories addressed at the sexual economy – Amsterdam's red light district. As mentioned previously in Chapter 5, red light districts afford men the ability to, after extensive window shopping, rent precisely the 'consumer item' they desire, and fuck 'it'. Sitting at a cafe and viewing such a scene affords one an ideal opportunity to see precisely the sort of women that men pay money to fuck when given a wide choice. There are women with pretty faces attached to very slim figures and women with pretty faces attached to pear-shaped figures and it is without doubt this latter group who do a brisk trade: the pears not the twigs. Many permutations remain to be explored. Crass as this may seem, it is a salutary lesson to those women obsessed with slimness. For men's erections and the subsequent issuing of their sperm, take not the slightest notion of the picture editors at *Vogue*. An erection is true to itself – a barometer of sexual truth in a world of aesthetic corruption. Such incorruptible aesthetes, full of sexual integrity, want to fuck what *they* want to fuck – trust their judgement.

It is important to point out that there are a number of other attributes which can also attract or repel men; however, these seem to live in the shadow of body shape. There is nothing like a pretty face to attract men. In fact, there is nothing like a pretty face to attract women, as exemplified by the front cover of every women's magazine. Those considering cosmetic surgery may first wish to know what, according to scientific studies, is seen to constitute a 'pretty' face. A number of studies carried out in societies as diverse as the Soviet Union, Brazil, and several hunting and gathering tribes, have found that both genders judge as most attractive, faces that are near the 'average', as average faces tend to be more symmetrical, reflecting a person's genetic 'normality' or health. However, other more recent cross-cultural studies have found that the most attractive female face generally had higher cheek bones, a thinner jaw and larger eyes relative to the size of the face. It also featured a relatively short distance between the mouth and chin and between the nose and mouth.

Anyone involved in radio advertising or radio broadcasting is well aware that voices paint provocative images of their owners: often sexual ones at that. Robert Graves in 'The Outward and Inward Ears', *Observations on Poetry*, observed: 'The outward ear is easily deceived. A beautiful voice can make magic even with bad or fraudulent poetry.' Many a radio listener has been dismayed to find that the unseen broadcaster, who for ages has served as the object of their fantasies, when confronted in the flesh, looks quite 'unrecognisable'. This same principle applies to the role that a woman's voice plays in making her sexually appealing to men. Some men are particularly attuned to and highly swayed by voice quality. Furthermore, the voices employed on the lewd 0898-telephone lines found in the back of many magazines and newspapers, are unlikely to bear any relation to the actual physical attractiveness of the speaker, yet they help desperate men reach millions of telephone-induced orgasms every year at 49 pence per minute, peak rate.

Britain has the added dimension of profound differences in social class and of regional variation in accent, both of which have an effect upon sexual attractiveness and, moreover, one's degree of 'marriageability'. When attempting to improve their marketability, British women do not, as a rule, tend to opt for elocution lessons in fluent Brummy nor attend evening classes to better familiarise themselves with the eloquent tones of 'Saiff-Eest' London enunciation. There is, however, a small proviso in the form of the sexual proclivities of the upper-class minister or senior civil servant who writhes at the sound of a 'filthy little working-class scrubber'. It is always rather amusing to witness educated Britons declaring obsequiously their undying love of Britain's 'rich variety of interesting accents and dialects'.

There are other less overt qualities that are terribly attractive to men but cannot be photographed, quantified or purchased. Caring, nurturing, comforting, maternalistic, and sympathetic characteristics are difficult to identify in any precise way, but to most men they reek of femininity and therefore have tremendous sexual appeal. Contemporary culture would, unfortunately, appear to take such qualities for granted, even thinking them somewhat mundane, sycophantic and passé – preferring to admire the more predatory and steely qualities promoted in recent times. None the less, vulnerability in a woman can still bring out more protective and caring qualities in a man. There remain many seemingly unremarkable women whose husbands are extravagantly handsome and desirable. Other women may, unfortunately, see them as somehow 'undeserving' and tongues wag behind their backs. The way a woman caresses can say much about her, as can her way of looking at a man, despite the fact that these subtleties don't make glamorous copy.

No doubt, while the perspective on slenderness presented above may have proved mildly interesting, few are likely to have altered their desire to lose weight or become thinner. Given that this is the case, there are further elements of confusion and distortion created by those sections of the 'self-improvement' market who provide information concerning the logistical aspects of achieving a change of form. If one is inclined to pursue slenderness, then it is important to be in possession of some fundamental truths about weight and body shape, spelled out in plain, simple English. Here are the facts: do with them what you will and on your own hips and thighs be it.

The first things to consider are the 'diagnostic' techniques employed to help women judge precisely how much they should hate themselves. Such self-judgement by numbers seems a rather tidy, accurate affair, however, women have been using the wrong numbers. The concept of weight has been out of date for some time and while many judge themselves by looking at the number of pounds on the scales, weighing yourself every morning doesn't really tell you very much and is misleading. For example, as muscle weighs more than fat, a fit woman who takes a size 12 in clothes can find herself weighing more than an unfit woman who takes size 14.

A scale doesn't tell you very much about your body *composition*

– how much of your body is made up of fat versus muscle and bone. Nor does it tell you much about your shape, where your fat is actually located. After all, how can one develop a proper self-hatred without being given the correct information to promote a more accurate form of self-detestation? Fat on hips, thighs, and bottoms is normal, healthy and a necessary factor in producing the hormones, such as oestrogen, that make women look and feel feminine. However, fat stored beneath the stomach muscles (intra-abdominal fat), is quite a different matter. It is linked to higher blood cholesterol levels, heart disease, a certain type of diabetes, high blood pressure, strokes, and a slightly increased risk of breast cancer. Middle-aged men are particularly at risk from this kind of fat and believe foolishly that when it comes to their waistline, 'if it doesn't wobble, it isn't fat'. A person's stomach can feel firm because the fat beneath the stomach muscles is stretching them as tight as piano strings.

And so the irony is that while it is women who are preoccupied with their size, weight and dieting, it is in reality men who need to be concerned about their eating, weight and health. Although they die prematurely from coronary heart disease at roughly four times the rate that women do, there is little scope for the self-improvement industry to make inroads on a gender more concerned about premature baldness and premature ejaculation.

Traditional methods of gauging whether a person's *weight* is appropriate, such as height/weight charts, have been replaced by a new method called *Body Mass Index* (BMI). The traditional 'height and weight' chart is based upon average weights of a sample population, usually people seeking life insurance, so they are only *average* weights, not *ideal* weights as is often assumed. Moreover, they ignore differences in bone structure and body composition. There is also a new method for determining whether someone has a healthy, attractive *shape*, called the

Waist-to-Hip Ratio (WHR). It is imperative to find both Body Mass Index and Waist-to-Hip Ratio to gain a clear picture of where one stands before setting about deconstructing one's physique.

BODY MASS INDEX CHART

While most scientists agree that a BMI over 40 is a serious health risk, there is some disagreement as to whether people with a BMI of 25 to, say, 31 have anything to be terribly concerned about. Generally, people with a BMI between 20 and 25 have a lower risk of many of the diseases already mentioned. People with a BMI between 25 and 30 have a 'moderate' risk, while those with a BMI over 30 have an increasingly greater risk. They are also at risk from diseases involving the joints and muscles, such as certain types of arthritis. People with a BMI below 20 have a greater risk of diseases as well, such as malfunction of their reproductive organs causing possible effects with their fertility, as well as severe depression, brittle bones and osteoporosis.

WAIST-TO-HIP RATIO CHART

A waist-to hip ratio greater than 0.8 for women and 0.95 for men indicates that they are storing too much intra-abdominal fat and this places them at increased risk of premature death. So while a woman's hips should be at least 20 per cent larger than her waist, a man's should be at least 5 per cent larger than his waist. Infertility is currently a prominent issue and recently it has been found, in a study published in the *British Medical Journal*, that body fat distribution, or body shape, might have some bearing on whether or not a woman has trouble conceiving. Women whose waist-to-hip ratios were greater

WAIST-TO-HIP RATIO CHART

Waist measurement in cm

Waist (cm)	Waist (in)	Hip cm → 63	66	69	71	74	76	79	81	84	86	89	91	94	96	99	102	104	107	109	112	114
		Hip in → 25	26	27	28	29	30	31	32	33	34	35	36	37	38	39	40	41	42	43	44	45
91	36	1.44	1.38	1.33	1.29	1.24	1.20	1.16	1.13	1.09	1.06	1.03	1.00	0.97	0.95	0.92	0.90	0.88	0.86	0.84	0.82	0.80
89	35	1.40	1.35	1.30	1.25	1.21	1.17	1.13	1.09	1.06	1.03	1.00	0.97	0.95	0.92	0.90	0.88	0.85	0.83	0.81	0.80	0.78
86	34	1.36	1.31	1.26	1.21	1.17	1.13	1.10	1.06	1.03	1.00	0.97	0.94	0.92	0.89	0.87	0.85	0.83	0.81	0.79	0.77	0.76
84	33	1.32	1.27	1.22	1.18	1.14	1.10	1.06	1.03	1.00	0.97	0.94	0.92	0.89	0.87	0.85	0.83	0.80	0.79	0.77	0.75	0.73
81	32	1.28	1.23	1.19	1.14	1.10	1.07	1.03	1.00	0.97	0.94	0.91	0.89	0.86	0.84	0.82	0.80	0.78	0.76	0.74	0.73	0.71
79	31	1.24	1.19	1.15	1.11	1.07	1.03	1.00	0.97	0.94	0.91	0.89	0.86	0.84	0.82	0.79	0.78	0.76	0.74	0.72	0.70	0.69
76	30	1.20	1.15	1.11	1.07	1.03	1.00	0.97	0.94	0.91	0.88	0.86	0.83	0.81	0.79	0.77	0.75	0.73	0.71	0.70	0.68	0.67
74	29	1.16	1.12	1.07	1.04	1.00	0.97	0.94	0.91	0.88	0.85	0.83	0.81	0.78	0.76	0.74	0.73	0.71	0.69	0.67	0.66	0.64
71	28	1.12	1.08	1.04	1.00	0.97	0.93	0.90	0.88	0.85	0.82	0.80	0.78	0.76	0.74	0.72	0.70	0.68	0.67	0.65	0.64	0.62
69	27	1.08	1.04	1.00	0.96	0.93	0.90	0.87	0.84	0.82	0.79	0.77	0.75	0.73	0.71	0.69	0.68	0.66	0.64	0.63	0.61	0.60
66	26	1.04	1.00	0.96	0.93	0.90	0.87	0.84	0.81	0.79	0.76	0.74	0.72	0.70	0.68	0.67	0.65	0.63	0.62	0.60	0.59	0.58
63	25	1.00	0.96	0.93	0.89	0.86	0.83	0.81	0.78	0.76	0.74	0.71	0.69	0.68	0.66	0.64	0.63	0.61	0.60	0.58	0.57	0.56
61	24	0.96	0.92	0.89	0.86	0.83	0.80	0.77	0.75	0.73	0.71	0.69	0.67	0.65	0.63	0.62	0.60	0.59	0.57	0.56	0.55	0.53
58	23	0.92	0.88	0.85	0.82	0.79	0.77	0.74	0.72	0.70	0.68	0.66	0.64	0.62	0.61	0.59	0.58	0.56	0.55	0.53	0.52	0.51
56	22	0.88	0.85	0.81	0.79	0.76	0.73	0.71	0.69	0.67	0.65	0.63	0.61	0.59	0.58	0.56	0.55	0.54	0.52	0.51	0.50	0.49
53	21	0.84	0.81	0.78	0.75	0.72	0.70	0.68	0.66	0.64	0.62	0.60	0.58	0.57	0.55	0.54	0.53	0.51	0.50	0.49	0.48	0.47
51	20	0.80	0.77	0.74	0.71	0.69	0.67	0.65	0.63	0.61	0.59	0.57	0.56	0.54	0.53	0.51	0.50	0.49	0.48	0.47	0.45	0.44
48	19	0.76	0.73	0.70	0.68	0.66	0.63	0.61	0.59	0.58	0.56	0.54	0.53	0.51	0.50	0.49	0.48	0.46	0.45	0.44	0.43	0.42

Hip measurement in cm · Hip measurement in inches

Waist measurement in cm

Note: Measure your waist at the level of your navel, then measure your hips at the greatest point around your bottom.

BODY MASS INDEX CHART

Height in feet and inches

Weight in pounds / Weight in kilograms

Height in metres

Height (m)	100	105	110	115	120	125	130	135	140	145	150	155	160	165	170	175	180	185	190	195	200	205	210	Height
(kg)	45	48	50	52	55	57	59	61	64	66	68	70	72	75	77	79	82	84	86	89	91	93	95	
1.83								18.2	19.1	19.7	20.3	20.9	21.5	22.4	23	23.6	24.5	25.1	25.7	26.6	27.2	27.8	28.4	6'
1.80							18.2	18.8	19.7	20.4	21	21.6	22.2	23.1	23.8	24.4	25.3	25.6	26.5	27.5	28	28.7	29.3	5'11"
1.78							18.6	19.2	20.2	20.8	21.5	22.1	22.7	23.7	24.3	24.9	25.9	26.5	27.8	28	28.7	29.3	29.9	5'10"
1.75						18.6	19.3	19.9	20.9	21.5	22.2	22.9	23.5	24.5	25.1	25.8	26.8	27.4	28.1	29.1	29.7	30.4	31	5'9"
1.73					18.4	19	19.7	20.4	21.4	22	22.7	23.4	24.1	25	25.7	26.4	27.4	28.1	28.7	29.8	30.4	31.1	31.8	5'8"
1.70					19	19.7	20.4	21.1	22.1	22.8	23.5	24.2	24.9	25.9	26.6	27.3	28.4	29.1	29.6	30.6	31.4	32.1	32.8	5'7"
1.68				18.4	19.5	20.2	20.9	21.6	22.7	23.4	24.1	24.8	25.5	26.6	27.3	28	29	29.8	30.7	31.8	32.5	33.2	33.9	5'6"
1.65			18.4	19.1	20.2	20.9	21.7	22.4	23.5	24.2	25	25.7	26.4	27.5	28.3	29	30.1	30.8	31.8	32.9	33.7	34.4	35.2	5'5"
1.63		18.1	18.8	19.6	20.7	21.4	22.2	23	24.1	24.8	25.6	26.3	27.1	28.2	29	29.7	30.9	31.6	32.3	33.4	34.2	34.9	35.7	5'4"
1.60		18.7	19.5	20.3	21.5	22.3	23	23.8	25	25.8	26.6	27.3	28.1	29.3	30.1	30.9	32	32.8	33.6	34.7	35.5	36.3	37.1	5'3"
1.58	18	19.2	20	20.8	22	22.8	23.6	24.4	25.6	26.4	27.2	28	28.8	30	30.8	31.6	32.8	33.6	34.2	35.4	36.2	37	37.8	5'2"
1.55	18.7	20	20.8	21.6	22.9	23.7	24.6	25.4	26.6	27.5	28.3	29.1	30	31.2	32	32.9	34.2	35	35.8	37	37.9	38.7	39.6	5'1"
1.53	19.2	20.5	21.4	22.2	23.5	24.3	25.2	26.1	27.3	28.2	29	29.9	30.8	32	32.9	33.8	35	35.9	36.7	38	38.9	39.7	40.6	5'
1.50	20	21.3	22.2	23.1	24.4	25.3	26.2	27.1	28.4	29.3	30.2	31.1	32	33.3	34.2	35.1	36.4	37.3	38.2	39.5	40.4	41.3	42.2	4'11"
1.48	20.5	21.9	22.8	23.7	25.1	26	26.9	27.8	29.2	30.1	31	32	32.9	34.2	35.2	36.1	37.4	38.3	39.2	40.6	41.5	42.4	43.4	4'10"

than 1.0 were less likely to become pregnant after artificial insemination. Furthermore, the bigger a woman's waist was in relation to her hips, the smaller her chances of conception. This finding reinforces the rationale for men preferring a more pear-shaped figure.

It is important to mention that while many may be tempted to entertain psychological interpretations as to why they have been eating more, gaining weight and changing body shape, the answers may lie within more mundane explanations. Scientists have observed that women, in response to seasonal changes, show big increases in muscle and bone mass during summer and autumn, and comparable decreases during winter and spring. Fat distribution also shifts with the seasons. During the winter, women carry around more fat, particularly in the legs and trunk. This is not because they may be less active. Other research has found that, on average, men and women eat about 220 more calories a day in the autumn – chiefly in the form of carbohydrates – than in any other season. Moreover, they feel hungrier after meals in the autumn than after eating in the spring, summer, or winter, despite the fact that they consume more calories. This may be the result of the body's mechanism for experiencing fullness being suppressed during the autumn, as some sort of legacy from prehistoric times when it was vital for people to fatten themselves up for long winters when food was scarce. Such an explanation either falls upon deaf ears or is ignored in favour of more 'sophisticated' reasoning.

A lack of understanding of the role of alcohol is also largely responsible for unwanted body fat. Most people assume that in some general way, 'drink is fattening' without realising precisely how fattening alcohol actually is – and why. Alcohol has nearly twice the calories of pure sugar, but it is now thought that alcohol also drastically reduces one's ability to burn dietary fat: it slows down one's metabolism. The liver, which normally burns fat, is suddenly distracted, finding itself too busy to process the alcohol, and the fat that would have been burned by the liver gets stored – usually in women's hips and thighs and in men's stomachs. Again there is a distinct lack of a psychological or even a 'foody' perspective to introduce here.

Genetics – the term hated by those promoting ideas of accessible change – appear to play an enormous role in programming some people to gain and maintain weight much more easily than others. While researchers are still busy investigating this concept intensively, everybody knows someone who eats enormous amounts of whatever they like and never seems to gain an ounce, and someone else who merely picks at their food yet still becomes fatter. The carefree eaters appear to have much faster metabolisms and body temperatures which are consistently higher, in some cases by as much as half a degree. In primitive times, such an 'attribute' would have been an expensive liability, but genetic predispositions of this kind blossom in Western industrialised societies where food is varied and plentiful and diets are high in fat; sugar, salt and flavour enhancers make food even more palatable, causing people to eat more; and many lead a sedentary life. Those with slow metabolisms have the perfect opportunity to show their potential. One's metabolic rate also decreases with age.

There is also the concept of the body's *set point* for retaining fat which is often compared to a thermostat of sorts in that it maintains a preselected amount of body fat. Some researchers believe that fatter people simply have a higher set point for body fat than thinner ones. Dieting is well known for making people irritable, miserable – and, of course, hungry. It is thought that these feelings are the body's set point crying out for acknowledgement. A classic study conducted at the University of Minnesota found not only the obvious – that not eating enough food causes psychological distress – but that underfed people continue to feel miserable until they return to their original weight. The subjects went on a semi-starvation diet for six months and were then given the opportunity to regain the weight they had lost. However, even several months after abandoning the diet, and despite eating enormous amounts of food, they remained ravenous and irritable. Only when they returned to their original weight did they feel better and stop gorging themselves. Support for the idea that a body's set point has feelings too.

There is further evidence that dieting has psychological, reproductive and sexual repercussions. Female brain chemistry in particular is altered quite significantly during dieting. Levels of neurotransmitters, which fend off depression, change in response to dieting – and not for the better. Dieting also affects intellect: it makes people less intelligent. While it is well known that in women who are underweight, periods can cease altogether, German researchers found that even the most conservative dieting was associated with much shorter menstrual cycles. Moreover, the scientists believe that when a woman diets, her body compensates for loss of energy by reducing hormone output. They found, for example, lower progesterone levels in women who diet. It is suspected that these effects reduce a woman's fertility. The greatest irony lies in the observation that, while women believe they will be more attractive as the result of dieting, the changes in hormone and neurotransmitter levels conspire to lead their libidos into decline.

Approximately one in four women is on a diet at any given time, yet the population is heavier than ever. The affluent and celebrated female role-models with a proclivity to pudginess, fail repeatedly and publicly to maintain their weight-losses, despite their vast financial resources. Even if women want to lose weight (despite the fact that they are of a normal weight or underweight), dieting is still the most unsuccessful method of deconstructing oneself unnecessarily. Whittle away your already underweight figure at your peril, but be aware that dieting is both an unsuccessful, yet a highly saleable, technique. Studies show consistently that any diet can enable people to lose weight – but none can enable them to keep it off. Most people gain the weight back within a year, often ending up fatter than they started. Furthermore, 'yo-yo dieting', a favourite pastime of many Western women, seems to damage their metabolism in ways that cause them to regain pounds even faster than they would normally. Some studies have shown that repeated weight gains and losses actually encourage fat storage. The respected, high-profile weight-loss organisations supply advertisements and client testimonials as 'information' which is then accepted uncritically by customers, yet these organisations won't allow independent scientific investigators to evaluate the real outcome of their weight-loss 'programmes'. What is most conspicuous by its absence is information regarding client drop-out rates and what level a person's weight returns to a year after enrolment.

Aside from inheriting favourable genes, there are only three major factors which can help lower one's Body Mass Index and Waist-to-Hip Ratio: reducing one's consumption of alcohol, increasing the amount of physical activity one engages in, and reducing the amount of fat one eats.

PHYSICAL ACTIVITY

People need two forms of exercise:

aerobic:
any continuous action movements using large muscle groups. This gives you more fat-burning compartments in your muscle cells so you will burn more food, even when you're not

exercising. Examples are brisk walking, dancing, cycling, skating, table tennis, cutting grass (using a push-mower), tennis, football, swimming, rowing, golf (as long as you walk the course).

anaerobic:
very much the opposite, requiring short bursts of intense energy. Examples are light-weight training, sprinting, sit-ups and press-ups. These build more muscle which is a 'hungry' tissue: one pound of muscle burns 30 to 50 calories per day just doing nothing, while the same weight of body fat burns only two. So the more muscle you have, the more fat and calories you burn just sitting down.

Moreover, aerobic activity seems to have a positive effect on the body's appetite-control mechanism, which can be weakened by an inactive lifestyle. Doing this sort of exercise, you are likely to make more intelligent food choices because your body will automatically set nutritional priorities to replace the lost nutrients, by making you eat healthier foods.

FOOD

Fat is a much richer source of calories ounce for ounce than either carbohydrate (starch) or protein. Furthermore, all calories are not equal. It seems that dietary fat comes in a form that can be stored effortlessly as body fat. Fat is also not the preferred energy source for your body to function most efficiently — carbohydrates are. Calories from carbohydrates, on the other hand, burn the fastest of all and aren't converted easily into body fat. So, 100 calories from margarine are more fattening than 100 calories from bread. Carbohydrates, particularly the wholegrain variety, are *not* in themselves fattening. They only become fattening when they are cooked or served with fat.

EATING

Snacking between meals, or 'grazing', has wrongly been thought of as fattening; whereas in fact it can help make people slimmer. Eating healthy food such as fruit, crisp breads and/or raisins between meals will help maintain blood sugar levels and help you make healthier choices at meal times. Skipping breakfast slows down metabolism and may also cause you to choose to eat more high-fat foods later on in the day. The slower metabolism combined with the poor food choices and additional fatty snacking can provide you with an extra half stone of body fat in a year. Giving your body reason to suspect that you may be depriving it of food will trigger its protective mechanism which, in turn, seeks and retains fat for storage. While it appears that by eating your biggest meal of the day at lunchtime, you are less likely to store as much of it as body fat, changing the tradition of large dinners to large lunches may be asking too much.

Observing the measures adopted by Japanese sumo wrestlers wishing to gain and retain weight provides an interesting insight into how the timing of their eating may play a role in the way civilians gain and retain their weight: and their gain could be your loss. The sumo diet isn't particularly rich or high in fat; however, sumo wrestlers eat most of their food in one or two large meals a day. All sumo wrestlers skip breakfast, and ironically, when they exercise on their large but empty stomachs, their metabolism actually slows down and ends up even lower than before. Normal exercise boosts metabolism but, in those who leave large gaps between meals, exercise is perceived as a threat to the body's fuel supplies so it slows down the metabolism as an act of self-protection. As is becoming increasingly obvious, eating between meals can be a remarkably sensible thing to do.

Many of the most obvious explanations of 'overeating' and

subsequent weight gain simply don't sell. However, by elevating the dynamics of eating to a cerebral level, we are given the impression that if eating involves a lot of thought, then, like many other things in the world of psychology, it too can be managed. And, of course, an inability to manage successfully is a 'failure'.

9: Working for a Change

Effecting organisational change through personal change provides the most lucrative example of the misappropriation of psychological concepts. Organisations, both public and private, spend hundreds of millions of pounds each year on the latest in new approaches, many of which are couched in psychological terms. Such endeavours would appear to be the organisational version of a mental make-over, with much effort being put into 'reinventing' and 'redefining' the organisation, and for each strand of the project ('strategic forward planning' – based, no doubt, upon a 'mission statement'), there is a term, e.g. 'Business Process Re-engineering'. However, it is the accommodation of 'change' that receives most attention.

What seems to escape those who chose to present 'change' as a desirable state of affairs is the fact that people on the whole do not particularly like change. They prefer routine and security. Moreover, if there is any change to be made, they prefer to initiate it themselves. Nevertheless, an entire industry has developed to 'help' employees better understand how positive and how much fun change can be!

The recessionary period of the early Nineties was heralded by the term 'change'. Books, courses, videos and management consultancies all exuding the requisite terms, surrounded and assisted in 'the process of change'. I was contacted by one organisation engaged in 'the process of change'. I met with the senior management at The Average Blue-Chip Corporation (ABC), and an interesting discussion ensued:

Snr Manager: So Dr Sigman, I hope you can join our team and assist us in the process of 'change'. Considering our position, what are your suggestions to 'facilitate' 'change'?

Me: What kind of 'change' are we talking about?

SM: Well, we at ABC have, through our 'mission statement', clarified our aim to achieve a more 'efficient', 'dynamic' organisation through 'creative restructuring'. As 'restructuring' involves 'change', we felt it best to ensure that such a 'transition' goes smoothly.

Me: What kind of 'creative restructuring' are we talking about?

SM: ABC feels that the organisation as a whole could benefit from a degree of 'Business Process Re-engineering' – the Americans seem to have embraced this concept very successfully and we want to be at the 'cutting edge' of 'corporate design' and hope to derive increased profitability as part of our long-term 'strategic plan'.

Me: What kind of 'Business Process Re-engineering' are we talking about?

SM: Well, it will involve 'right-sizing', affording some of our employees with the opportunity of pursuing new beginnings. While for others, there's the need for 'adaptation' to their exciting new roles. There are opportunities for everyone here. We're all looking to the future.

Me: Oh, now I understand. You're going to make a lot of people redundant.

SM: Well, off the record and entirely *entre nous*, Dr Sigman, ABC will be making some workforce adjustments. Redundancies if you like. But it will leave us leaner and meaner and in a much stronger, more competitive position for the future, benefiting everyone here.

Me: And those remaining employees?

SM: They need to feel *good* about the company and their new and improved roles within it. It's a question of setting the right frame of mind. The sooner everyone's happy, the quicker we can fully engage in the cut and thrust of healthy competition in the new world markets.

Me: So, to summarise, you're going to be firing lots of people and you want me to help them view their redundancy as a 'positive opportunity'. At the same time, you want me to assist the survivors – who will have to work twice as hard – to view this 'creative restructuring' as a seaside holiday, not as clinging to the lifeboat wondering if the sharks are going to get them next.

SM: Dr Sigman, there's no need to put it like that – *I* didn't get where I am today by . . .

Terminology is central to contemporary management and such corporate-speak is not reserved for couching bad news in pretty parcels, for it can be applied to all manner of things: 'stress management', 'assertiveness training', 'neurolinguistic programming' or 'managing change'. There are even more overt attempts at corporate self-improvement with the first management book ever to rank No. 1 on the American national best-seller list, the best-selling business book of all time, entitled

In Search of Excellence, and a subsequent book bearing the title *A Passion for Excellence*, also becoming a No. 1 non-fiction best-seller. A competitor's offerings come in the form of an audio-cassette programme entitled *Excellence in Action* by Buck Rogers. Buck, we are told, 'shares with you the core values, concepts and ideas . . . Now you can: Find out how to make excellence "come alive" in any organisation. Employ fundamentals and sophisticated techniques . . .'

Those who had failed to find excellence when searching for it, may find solace by skimming through the pages of *Downsizing Without Disaster*. When firing people, companies find it necessary to dilute the implications by invoking further specialist corporate-speak to soften the blow, rather like the way we euphemise death by the corporate equivalent of the CIA's term for assassination, 'to terminate without prejudice'. The introduction of *Downsizing Without Disaster* informs one that, 'Losing employees – terminating people – isn't fun': Mr Schwarzenegger of course may take issue with this. This book provides a good overview of how management consultancies can provide terminology to address all human life. One is informed that 'Both managers and employees have feelings. . . . Employee morale snaps like a whiplash victim. . . . It is often a very bumpy ride.' One is encouraged to 'demonstrate sympathy and empathy . . . you should maintain a positive tone and use appropriate humour' – even though they don't tell you how to deal with a down-siz*ee* who doesn't find it funny. However, the unsympathetic down-siz*er* is cautioned not to 'insult employees [with phrases like] we just got rid of some deadwood'. Those managers wishing to 'use appropriate humour' can refer to another offering by the same publishers, entitled *Making Humour Work*.

Lucy Kellaway of the *Financial Times*, after writing about large-scale redundancies, was inundated 'by scores of consultants specialising in the "survivor syndrome"'. One such,

Alternative International, has sent me a 12-page fax explaining how these employees need to be "emotionally reconnected to the employer" via three-day workshops consisting of "force field analysis" and an "external environment review". This cure sounds almost as painful as the disease – and not everyone wants to be emotionally connected to their employer.'

One key term, central to psychology, is that of 'communication'. Individuals have, for some time, been encouraged to 'communicate' more. This concept, however, has also been adopted at a corporate level whereby organisations as a whole are expected to 'communicate' with various departments and employees in general. Recently, there has been greater emphasis on the importance of communication going in *both* directions, particularly from 'below stairs' employees to those of the upper echelons. With this in mind, a process referred to as 'Upward Feedback' has been developed, which invites employees to tell their bosses exactly what they think of them. This is achieved through first filling in confidential forms and then facing the boss directly in a form of post-mortem. This is how the procedure is likely to work in practice:

Snr Manager: So, Employee, we at ABC have decided to implement an improved system of communication because we want to know what *you*, whose valuable input makes ABC the successful company it is today, think of *us*.

Employee: Um, yes?

SM: No need to beat about the bush – we're all part of one big team.

E: Well, um, I've never really thought about it.

SM: You must have *some* thoughts on the matter. Tell me what you think about me as your boss. Don't be shy. It's confidential, you know.

E: You *really* want to know?

SM: Yes of course. Come on, spit it out.

E: Well, actually . . .

SM: Yes?

E: Er. Well, I suppose you could be less . . .

SM: Yes? Less what?

E: Er. Less, um, perhaps, shall I say enthusiastic about the company.

SM: What on earth are you talking about? We're *supposed* to be enthusiastic – it's *our* company. All for one and one for all. Enthusiasm is central to ABC's success.

E: Yes, I know enthusiasm is an important part of my job, but . . .

SM: And it's a job we all enjoy!

E: I'm glad ABC is so successful and I do want to play my part, but, quite frankly, I and my colleagues wish you didn't get so fired up about it. It's a bit taxing.

SM: Taxing? It's ennobling! I go on all these courses to find out how to run things better and it's *my* job to transfer my enthusiasm to *you*. So, come on, come on. We can be adult about this. Tell me what you *really* think.

E: Um ... if you put it that way ... *actually*, I think you're an *asshole*! A management lackey. You brown-nose the MD and expect us to do the same to you – well, all I can say is, don't hold your breath, mate. There. Does that help, sir?

SM: Um ... Er ... well ... thank you for your honesty, Employee. Of course, I'd like to assure you that I will carefully consider your comments when we're working on our new Business Process Re-engineering programme. When we finalise our plans, *you'll* be the first to know. Good day.

Lucy Kellaway has seen the wood for the trees: 'There are plenty of seminars that promise to turn bumbling managers into world-class communicators. But there is a sad lack of more modest courses which accept that inept people are not going to change, and instead offer them advice on how to extricate themselves from the regrettable situations into which they stumble.' While in another article, she reports that, 'The Management Training Partnership's research of UK personnel directors found that three-quarters of them buy at least four heavy-weight management books a year, but only one in five of these volumes stands any chance of being read.' She remarks: 'The message to writers and publishers is that if they want their books to be read, as well as sold, the style cannot be too downmarket, and the argument cannot be summarised too briefly, nor in big enough letters. So far, the lesson has not been learnt: few books contain summaries. The problem may be that if you condense the arguments in many management books too ruthlessly, you would be left with simple statements of the glaringly obvious.'

Management development is not reserved for 'dry' organisations. In addition to making the world's most celebrated cartoons, Disney also has a university – Euro-Disney University – which publishes a 'Manager's Guide' entitled *Leadership Disney Style*. While executives at Disney are fortunately spared the indignity of donning mouse ears whilst engaging in management by walkabout, they are expected to adopt other Californian-derived philosophies. They are first informed 'The Disney style of leadership is not a mould you are expected to fit into.' However, this suggestion is immediately contradicted by the next sentence: 'Rather, it is a basic approach to management that allows you to express your own personality while practising the fundamentals of Disney leadership that have been proven to produce high quality results. Your mission is clear . . . This book is for you. Use it often.' Another section promotes 'dreaming and doing . . . the trademark of our management style and wise counsel for your Disney career. Be a dreamer . . . and a doer.' Wishing on a star?

McDonald's, the well-known fast-health-food giant, with their now infamous 'Have A Nice Day' and other selected forms of burger-derived positive thinking, is probably the company that first comes to mind when thinking of organisations which take 'communication' most seriously. While much has been made of the apparent insincerity of this script-speak, the truth is that it actually *does* work in the right context: the sun-belt of the United States. However, McDonald's in the UK has discovered, much to its chagrin and only through 'research', that such well-intentioned Yankee-Doodlisms seem somewhat out of place in the world's capital of 'service with a sneer' by recalcitrant Subjects who have consistently displayed a highly developed inability to distinguish between providing *service* and being *servile*. Like many aspects of British culture, it all comes back to the class system in the end, and while the recalcitrants are quite happy to wear the baseball caps, having to say 'thank you, please call again' is asking too much. However, McDonald's has taken note of this and has been busy training its 550 restaurant managers to be more 'flexible' and 'responsive' to local needs. In order to make communication a somewhat more personal affair, the use of colloquialisms and dialects will be allowed. If deemed appropriate by managers, McDonald's customers may be greeted by phrases such as 'Eh-up chuck' or 'Get that down your neck' or 'Here's your Big Mac, whack.' Strangely, McDonald's USA has shown little interest in training *their* employees to adopt such cosy import-speak.

Of course, communication can work to your advantage. Sarah, the Debbie McGee of *New, Improved,* told me of her own experiences with new and improved corporate communications. A company she had been with for a number of years decided to implement some of the new management techniques and set up employee appraisals. Having been told what to expect in her appraisal, Sarah became rather apprehensive that the amount of time she spent gossiping in the loo had been brought to her boss's attention. However, to her amazement, her lavatorial efforts were instead reconceptualised, and she found herself being *commended* on her 'interdepartmental communication skills' and for passing on valuable information about the work being done by other departments.

In making certain forms of communication a 'trainable' offence, the issue of sexual harassment has become a prominent feature within the codes of practice of more and more organisations. There are expensive corporate videos available to educate companies, for example, a series entitled *Pest Control*. While it is of course terribly important to address the issue of genuine sexual harassment, such concern has had other, rather unfortunate repercussions for the core of office life. Organisations thrive upon energy, and an unmentioned and unmentionable part of this is sexual energy. Furthermore, one of the few things that makes work tolerable is the prospect of a social life, and for some that social life means finding a romantic partner. Given the current emphasis on 'communication', it is rather short-sighted of companies to attempt to eradicate the most long-standing form of communication – the *frisson*. As Katharine Hadley argues: 'In this country we suffer from a terrible prudishness about this sort of thing. Using one's sex appeal to get to the top just isn't politically correct, so we ignore it – which is pretty stupid, because people will always do it. Besides, sexuality is only an adjunct to talent and brains, not a substitute. In real life you can never sleep with the producer and get the lead role, unless, of course, you can act. Getting there is one thing, staying there quite another.' Some would say that flirting is the official job description for Public Relations work. Researchers such as Professor Cary Cooper believe that 'at work, sexuality is all around us. It influences decision-making, who is hired, who is listened to in meetings. It is conveyed by the subtlest of messages, a touch on the shoulder, the borrowing of a pen.' Another example of a corporate attempt at 'emotion management'.

One particular term, 'time management', whilst not being derived from psychology, has implications for psychology. In the way that some people do not have a feel for dealing with their finances, there are others who do not have a feel for the currency of time, its minutes and hours. Such a characteristic is deeply ingrained, probably even inborn, part of one's personality, one's identity, one's self. Like the idea of 'managing emotions', or changing personality, any notion of seriously influencing one's ability to manage time is bound to fail. One normally finds that those who are already good at time management can refine this aptitude by some of the specific information and products available, whilst those timeless individuals who aren't, are highly unlikely to change much at all. Anyone must realise that, even with the advent of the Filofax, the digital watch and its wretched alarm, and the electronic personal organiser, friends of ours who were, in the pre-digital era, habitually irresponsible and late, continue to be so.

Recently, the concept of 'empowerment' has crossed over into a corporate context, the idea being that an empowered employee is a happy employee. However, there seems to be some confusion as to precisely what 'empowered' actually means in practical terms. Peter Senge, of the MIT Sloane School of Management, speaks of 'this fad of empowerment . . . What they mean by empowerment varies dramatically . . . many of them are really talking about firing middle management.' A definition no doubt welcomed by quite a few employees.

There are other approaches to management development which are couched in more scientific terms, such as 'Brain Mapping for the Nineteen-Nineties' where one is informed that, with the appropriate training, the brain actually improves with age – and at an ever-accelerating rate. These claims, however, appear to run utterly contrary to what is generally known about the limitations that biology and, more specifically, ageing, places on learning and performance, or on changing personality and behaviour. Impressive schools of thought with labels such as 'Neuro-Linguistic Programming' (NLP) misappropriate psychological terminology and fatten it up for the market. Any doubts as to the validity of these philosophies are easily lost in a cacophony of management consultancy dogma, self-improvement lingo and corporate-speak. When corporations finally come to the conclusion that such approaches are a part of the emperor's invisible wardrobe, they simply fall prey to the next outbreak of management fashion – 'Total Quality Management' (TQM), 'Dimensional Management Feedback', 'Cross-Functional Team

Building', 'Intensive Influencing Skills'. There is, however, much to be said for the placebo effect of employees feeling that at least some money is being spent on giving them a day away from their desk. Moreover, management development is tax deductible.

'Stress management' is probably the best example of psychology being packaged and marketed by those outside the profession, for few courses on stress management are actually conducted by psychologists. Management consultants have dominated the field with buzz words and 'sure fire' methods, promising success in the fight to 'beat' stress. Some approaches to stress management include attempts to change personality and modes of thinking. However, one obstacle which is still prevalent in many organisations is the use of the term 'stress', for it implies, particularly for male employees, an admission of weakness – a quality which they assume will not impress the personnel department. With this in mind, much creative effort has gone toward camouflaging the intention of stress management courses, and this has been easily achieved through alternative terminology. For example, employees experiencing stress whilst waiting for the next round of redundancies to be made public are afforded courses on 'Managing Uncertainty'.

One particular form of stress, the Disaster, has proved a rather remunerative affair for more than just journalists and office equipment suppliers. For instance, the Bishopsgate bombing, coupled with threats of more to come, naturally caused many City employees some anxiety about going to work every day. A colleague of mine was asked by one international management consultancy to speak to a group of City bankers in order to inform them how to persuade their employees not to be concerned about being blown up in the future. He, however, suggested what he felt provided a more relevant line of discussion, that of Post Traumatic Stress Syndrome; a subject he was quite willing to talk about – as long as the venue was not in the City.

Much management development and customer service train-ing is merely a panacea for people who are not very good with people, who are usually promoted to the level of their own incompetence. In many cases it is also a substitute for a pay rise. This backdrop is itself underpinned by a class system which translates into the need for hierarchies in the workplace and a culture which has made disagreeable service an art form, and, in the case of *Fawlty Towers*, a television series. The notion of 'teamwork' defies the class-ridden cultural characteristics of Britain, but no amount of abseiling is going to overcome centuries of feudalism.

Susan Wood, of Communicate Consultancy Ltd in Britain, herself a management consultant, has some serious reservations about both the motivations of some managers who call in management consultancies, as well as the standards displayed by some outfits within her field:

What we find is that managers often appear to opt out of involving themselves in people development itself. This may take various forms, for example, the managers sending the employees on courses but not attending these courses or involving themselves in any way, yet expecting the trainers to simply 'produce the goods' for them. What many management consultancies and training organisations fail to recognise is that the same principles that apply to teaching school children – consideration of learning things through one of a number of ways, for example, pictorial Vs aural Vs written, is overlooked by trainers who have a mass-prescribed vision of what people should be taught, and an assumption that they will all be able to learn through the same technique. Anyone with children will realise that some children respond better to picture learn-ing, others to interactive experience and so on. Any personnel director is inundated with a plethora of impressive corporate brochures offering prescriptive, off-the-shelf courses which do not take into consideration individual characteristics of either the employees, the organisation or the other factors which must be looked at to achieve what the course claims it will achieve, for example, any talk of 'helping managers to manage change' must address not only the managers themselves but many other aspects of the corporate culture.

The recent trend in outdoor style learning has led many to suspect that the physical pursuits of the outdoors may possibly have little to do with the inner sanctum of corporate headquarters. This suspicion is certainly supported when considering that some companies running these courses have impressive physical backgrounds, i.e. SAS, ex-services etc, but have probably never stepped into either a business suit or a boardroom. Susan Wood notes that, 'It is vital to integrate and relate principles addressed on such courses directly back to issues within the organisation and this requires people who understand both worlds': canoes and companies. There seems to be little public concern about the application of group therapy psychology to organisations, particularly the type that has grown out of the 'primal scream' era, whereby in order for people to achieve a 'breakthrough', they are essentially broken down in front of their colleagues and may be left in such a state without the help of experienced people to deal with the consequences of their public breakdown. Moreover, in Britain, even the rumour that someone has broken down and cried can be devastating to their career and to their personal pride, and there is obviously a need to ensure that support, not only for the breakdown itself but also for the embarrassment that obviously ensues when the tears stop flowing, continues once that person returns to the office.

Eager young consultants looking for new ways to improve

employee morale and loyalty may, perhaps, be interested to know of a newly identified gap in the market. It is a truth, universally acknowledged by, amongst others, vending machine suppliers and women, that people working in offices are very fond of chocolate. To date, however, this observation seems to have escaped the attention of those management consultants who are normally prone to capitalising upon creating improved satisfaction and productivity through the conventional types of business games. The course outline would be as follows:

Monday 9.00am Delegates are whisked away from their head-quarters on their way by private luxury coach to the Willy Wonker Training Centre where they are met by their course leaders, Yorkie and Hershey, who introduce them to Phase One.

Monday 1.00pm Phase One. A three-course lunch prepared personally by Keith Floyd. Lunch is followed by Phase Two.

Monday 3.00pm Phase Two. Pudding – a comprehensive choice of chocolate puddings to be followed by Phase Three.

Monday 4.00pm Phase Three. Delegates will be driven to their five-star hotel for practical training in Siesta Management.

Monday 6.00pm Phase Four. Improved networking through role play involving pre-dinner cocktails.

Monday 7.30pm Coronation Street.

Monday 8.00pm Five-course dinner prepared personally by the Roux Brothers.

Monday 10.00pm After-dinner mints and speech on 'Sex, Chocolate & Desire'. Speaker to be announced.

Monday 11.00pm Delegates will be carried to their rooms by convivial staff, where they may avail themselves of the colour TV, bathroom gratuities and any other extras they require.

Tuesday 9.30am Breakfast.

Tuesday 10.30am Phase Five. Delegates will be driven back to the Willy Wonker Training Centre for a seminar on chocolate manufacturing.

Tuesday 10.35am Phase Six. A guided tour of the factory affording delegates the opportunity to get closer to and more fully appreciate the final product.

Tuesday 5.30pm Weight management and course assessment.

10: Radical Chic with Excuses for Sale

Psychology has been invoked through political movements to help 'improve' society. The left, having lost ground in both America and Britain as a result of 'Reaganism' and 'Thatcherism', turned away from the traditional political battlegrounds of class and economics, and concerned itself increasingly with more personal issues such as race, gender, sexual behaviour and orientation, and the educational curriculum. It chose to wage war, not in the main political arena, but in enclaves where it still retained some influence: local government, the subsidised sector of the Arts and, of course, the university campus. The fall-out from this has found its way into all forms of media.

One manifestation of this heady blend of 'civil rights' psychology has been the reinforcement of the notion of 'victimhood' whereby anyone who feels in some way marginalised can begin a new career as a 'former alcohol abuser', 'former substance abuser', 'former offender' or simply by being black – and psychology is right there behind them. This age has been encapsulated by a small leader article in the *Economist* entitled 'Sufferers All: America's Cult of Victimhood Means Never Having To Say You're Sorry':

> Victimhood, with its attendant court of psychiatrists and trauma detectors, is not entirely new; the whole political correctness industry is rooted in it.
>
> Suddenly, there are victims all over America; and they are not the dead, the wounded or the bruised, but the people on

the other side. Two blacks bash in the head of a white lorry driver with a brick, dance a little jig of joy, and are acquitted; they have been unreasonably provoked by the court verdict in the Rodney King case. It will not be long, at this rate, before the mandatory sentence for a crime of violence is a hug and a good cry.

As it is tolerated in the criminal courts, victimhood has become an excuse for irresponsibility and, at worst, for criminal acts. It implies that victims have a tendency, even a right, to behave in ways that hurt others. This is not only a slur against all those 'victims' who, despite provocation, struggle on and behave with unerring decency. It is also an almost wilful celebration of moral equivalence: that one bad thing may equal any other bad thing, and that two wrongs make a right.

It is interesting to note that the more privileged individual, such as Jamie Blandford – aristocrat, high-speed driver, drinker and pharmaceutical expert – with a catalogue of crimes and anti-social behaviour, would appear to have the perfect opportunity for invoking psychological excuses, but doesn't use them. What a shame: all the legal fees that could be saved. On the other hand, those below the law and their lawyers are very reluctant to pass up such opportunities.

It isn't only the *Untermenschen* who have benefited by pointing to their 'rights'. The late John Osborne, when speaking of the lower middle classes – the 'LMCs' – noted that 'a whole generation of barbarous, self-styled "Brits" has emerged, schooled to take pride in their ignorance and lustreless imagination, but rapacious in the appropriation of their "rights". There can be no closing the gap. Venom and envy, masquerading as equality.'

Young people are also into relativism and their rights. An amusing example of this growing trend in the young's interest in individualism and self-expression was played out on *Don't Forget Your Soapbox*, Channel 4's attempt at 'yoof' television. Viewers were treated to the sight of hand-picked representatives of the youth of today 'in conversation with' several token adults, with the programme being run by two teenagers who were no doubt chosen because of their ethnically challenged appearance and non-middle-class accents. The yoof, being au fait with current libertarian lingo, kept referring back to their 'rights', to do what they want and to be taught what they want in school. One particular teenager spoke up and, because of his strong regional accent, it was extremely difficult to understand what he was saying. The adult he was addressing kindly asked him to repeat himself and added that, speaking of rights, one of *his* rights was to be able to speak in a way which was clearly understandable to most people. This comment produced an outcry (in translation): 'You're discriminating against our accents – I'm proud of my colloquialisms,' and continued, 'what about our right to express ourselves?'

The left, which gained power in the inner cities in the 1980s, thought it knew best: anyone who disagreed, needed re-education – including the voters. David Selbourne, author of *The Principle of Duty*, who was a Marxist lecturer in the 1970s, states: 'Middle-class intellectuals who had turned themselves into honorary proletarians, found themselves arguing for policies which the beneficiaries did not want.' As the public image of these people was caricatured – convincingly portrayed in, for instance, Alan Bleasdale's *GBH* – such ideas had to be redirected instead through the media – a more fertile area for the promotion of the 'right' ideas.

An influential group of people (documentary makers and feature writers with attitude), appears to be in the advantageous position of interpreting news and making documentaries as a form of therapy for their personal hatreds and resentments and their need to patronise and, in a paternalistic way, fight for the rights of 'minority groups'. The image the women portray often appears to be a kind of cartoon style of femininity: strong lipstick, large earrings, a subtle kind of hip urban fashion (usually 'distressed', 'abused' and faded 501s with Doc Martens or knee-length army boots), and dyed hair for more of a man-made, urban style; at times almost a 'Gothic Playschool' effect made possible through their 'Camden Market Gold Card'. The feminine components of their dress, however, are not there to complement a feminine nature, but to convey an in-your-face, aggressive and sometimes butch attitude. It's a token nod to Bohemia: social awareness combined with sensitivity toward the needs of the oppressed who they hope will look up to them when in need. Their attitude is often reflected in the location of the film company for whom they work. One such film company, which is immensely successful, chooses to do business from a former factory next door to a railway bridge. However, the fun starts as you leave the tube station to enjoy a ten-minute stroll which takes you down a cold, ugly, desolate road, lined with old warehouse factories; trees aren't allowed in case they give the wrong impression – that one is in suburbia – but it's not Tim Burton's vision of Gotham City, it's Kentish Town. Stating their position, or positioning their statement?

While these people are so terribly concerned about improving the conditions for those less fortunate than themselves, it is rather curious that in such a 'caring' profession, charity most certainly does not begin at home, for they show few signs of empathy, are highly judgemental, confrontational, unsympathetic and dismissive. Many of them live in places like Brixton, which provide them with a combination of all the various elements necessary for a politically justified existence: plenty of underprivileged blacks who, interestingly, never seem to be invited over for supper; a South London urban postcode but which manages to retain the telling 0171 telephone non-bourgeois prefix; a healthy mix of 'ethnic' fruit and veg at the market as well as a well-stocked M&S over the road; copies of *The Big Issue* and *The*Newspaper tucked under their arm; and let us not forget the cheap rents made possible by the displacement of some of the black community which used to live there before their 'rescuers' arrived. In fact, figures compiled by the Housing Corporation's report, 'Approved Development Programme', show clearly that this is precisely what they have done. Despite their claims that Brixton is no more intimidating than any other part of London, it is interesting to observe their rather hurried pace when they leave Brixton tube late at night – doing the Lambeth Walk? Yet they could feel politically uncomfortable living in any other part of London. When they speak, they arrogantly assume that everyone present naturally subscribes to the same political and social views. They are genuinely shocked when they find that one doesn't. Dissent is not tolerated and non-conformists are either dismissed forthwith, or 'put right' in no uncertain terms. They could probably do a documentary about their abused and distressed black 501s if they thought there would be any political currency in it.

There was one particular occasion that stands out as an example of their brand of misappropriated psychology being rubbed in my face. The setting was a 'transmission' party, whereby the members of a documentary team get together at the producer's home to watch the transmission of their newly created masterpiece. Upon my arrival, I was told that it was a shame I missed the last transmission party for a programme involving heavy drug dealing as 'there were *real* Yardies doing *real* heavy drugs upstairs, and lots of dancing!'. At this, less adventurous party, I sat next to a woman who had short spiky hair and large earrings. She asked me what I did and I told her I was a psychologist. She must have wrongly assumed that, being

201

a psychologist, I would be *her* kind of psychologist: the kind who provides her clients with the excuses they need. I reciprocated by asking her whether she was in some way associated with the documentary being broadcast that evening, whereby she informed me that she was, in fact, a civil liberties lawyer who often appeared in Channel 4 documentaries to give a fair and objective opinion. The conversation then proceeded as follows:

Lawyer: You'd think civil liberties were improving, wouldn't you, but in fact things are getting worse. What's *really* needed are a few more riots like those in Brixton to make people sit up and take notice. If you think about it, violence is the only thing that helps create social change and improvement. Look at the Palestinians, for instance, or what's happened in South Africa, as opposed to what's happened to the Kurds.

Me: I can see your point, but violence cuts both ways, and this is a very dangerous path to tread. Say, for example, someone living in central London has had their flat broken into several times by blacks . . .

Lawyer: Don't use that term!

Me: What did I do wrong?

Lawyer: You should say 'black people' – they don't like being called 'blacks'.

Me: But the black people that I know, refer to their group as 'blacks' . . . however, if it bothers you, I'll change it. Anyway, as I was saying, if someone living in central London has had their flat broken into several times by black people, and decided that the way to create their own social change and improvement in the burglary statistics, was to get a gun and shoot any suspicious looking black people in the vicinity, you'd condone that as well, would you?

Lawyer: That's not the same thing – that would be racism.

Me: So, unlike black people, when white people use unlawful targeted violence, that's racism. Are you implying that black people can't be racist?

Lawyer: Black people suffer terrible racism in our society. Can you imagine what it must be like to be stopped by the police five times a day just because you're a black person?

Me: You still haven't answered my question. Can black people be racist too?

Lawyer: Almost all cases of racism that I've come across are committed by *white* people.

Me: Have you ever heard of the rap group Niggaz With Attitude?

Lawyer: You shouldn't use that word.

Me: They aren't my words, that's what they call themselves, and they're black. Sorry, black people.

Lawyer: Yes. So what's your point?

Me: You may be interested in some of the non-racist lyrics in

one of their singles called 'Fuck the Police'. I'll apologise for
my language in advance, but the song goes something like
this – 1, 2, a 1, 2, 3, 4: 'Hey motherfucker, I'm a nigger on the
warpath and when I'm done there's gonna be a blood bath'.
And there's another good, non-racist song by Public Enemy if
you'd like to hear it . . .

Lawyer: No, that's enough. So what's your point?

Me: My point is that racism cuts both ways.

Lawyer: But it's the *whites* who are really racist.

Me: Well, actually, I was part of the great 'integration' policy
in the States in the late 1960s which was an idea developed by
educationalists, psychologists and civil liberty lawyers, funnily
enough. They thought that familiarity would breed affection
and, to help people be more affectionate toward each other,
they moved black kids to predominantly white schools and
vice versa. Coming from a race which only twenty-five years
previously had been made into lampshades, I instinctively felt
I had a degree of sympathy with the 'victims of racism', and I
looked forward to forming new, two-tone friendships. So there
I was on my first day, enthusiastic and ready to bond, only to
be greeted with 'you white motherfucking cock sucker'. Over
that year, this description was fortunately softened to 'you
white pig'. So, tell me, how many black people did you go
to school with?

Lawyer: Um . . . there was one . . . or was it two?

Me: I don't suppose they were working-class black people,
were they?

Lawyer: No.

After lecturing me on the distinction between 'racism' and 'racialism', and examining my views on a wide variety of other sensitive issues, she concluded the interview by throwing down her knife and fork and declaring loudly: 'I can't believe it. You're a racist, a sexist and homophobic. You need to see a psychologist – you need help.' It was at this point that I wisely decided not to enlighten her any further as to the additional examples of 'reverse racism' on offer, in particular the street term of endearment developed *by* blacks to describe a black man who chooses to promote racial integration through having sexual liaisons with white women – a 'pig fucker'.

After hearing this supposed 'libertarian' so publicly describe me as a racist, I felt very angry and humiliated and so, in an attempt to seek absolution, I rang a ('some of my best *friends* are black!') black friend the next day to hear her thoughts on the matter of 'racism' Vs 'racialism' and 'blacks' Vs 'black people'. I was rather taken aback by her furious tirade against what she described as 'these modern-day missionaries who feel worthy and protective because they treat us like pets'. Jane, who lives in Islington, has had extensive experience of people concerned with assisting her into a career as a professional 'victim', and many of these 'caring' people happen to work in the media. She appeared to have had a bellyful of the missionaries' attempts to 'empower' her, to help her express her 'anger against racism', and to arrogantly assume she has some affinity with black *Untermenschen* – in other words, they deny her her right to be a middle-class black, and worse yet, her right to be a middle-class snob, just like whites. Having a penchant for smoked salmon and champagne, to be consumed preferably within the confines of Harvey Nichols, Jane finds their presumptive enthusiasm for 'ethnic' cuisine nothing short of irritating. 'Once they find out I prefer Glyndebourne to the Brixton Academy, they think I've sold out, and they drop me.'

Jane put her finger on the crux of the matter, for much of what has been described as 'racism' is actually 'classism'. Few of these caring libertarians would have any reservation in making judgements about young white men with shaved heads and tattoos. However, any mention of black men as being the same type of *Untermenschen* is considered to be racist. Such men can only be victims who are not particularly responsible for their actions, and they need to be supported, excused and empowered by their white libertarian protectors. She has particular disdain for those concerned whites who feel a deep need to patronise the Notting Hill Carnival, described as 'street anthropologists and bourgeois ravers'. However, her strongest vehemence is reserved for 'those media white bitches who, to feel good about themselves because they can't get fucked rigid by a white man, go off to Jamaica for a few weeks to hang out with a "Rent-a-Dread". Then they can pretend they're really concerned about our plight. If they're really so concerned about "integration" and "racism",' she continued, 'why is it that when they get pregnant by a black man in this country, they often end up having an abortion?' A clear case of failing to put your ovaries where your mouth is.

The confusion between racism and classism has a third dimension in which I became embroiled when I was involved with a ('some of my best *friends* are psychologists') psychologist from Trinidad who was *very* black; she was also a middle-class academic working in a university in New York State. On campus, attempts by white, so-called 'liberals' to court her, politically, or to assist her in cultivating a personal sense of chronic social injustice seemed alien to her, making her feel uncomfortable. However, she was also frustrated at the fact that many black

206

Americans seemed to resent her educated, 'empowered' status and that she found herself in the somewhat perplexing position of having only white, apolitical friends, as they seemed to accept her more readily.

Jane's observations mirror those of Ken Hamblin, the black American and *middle-class* radio broadcaster who expresses nothing but vitriol for 'poverty pimps, affirmative-action blacks, and egg-sucking dog white liberals who decriminalise crime'. In an attempt to redress any unnecessary white remorse for the fate of blacks, Mr Hamblin has a far more effective method of dealing with chronic guilt than self-help or psychotherapy: he now hands out 'Absolution From White Guilt' certificates.

Such reverence for victimhood was used to great effect when hip, social-change television really got underway several years ago in the form of 'yoof' programmes, in particular BBC 2's *Network 7*. One episode was concerned with the phenomenon of 'creepers': young, underprivileged men who, feeling disenfranchised and unempowered, take it upon themselves to quietly break into the homes of white, middle-class people while they are asleep, in order to walk about, invade their territory and to feel empowered by such covert action. Viewers were able to enjoy an interview with a black creeper, who smugly and proudly extolled the virtues of his craft, justifying himself with statements like, 'These people don't *care* about anybody else, they're just happy to earn lots of cash for themselves, they don't *care* about anyone else except themselves.' The implication was that, unlike these horrible white middle-class people, *he* would be terribly caring if he was as rich as they were. A strong indication of his caring nature was made clear when asked what he does if someone wakes up and discovers him creeping around their house: 'I carry a knife and I know where to stab someone so it stops them but doesn't kill them.' All of this took place to the sound of the latest hip music supplemented by freeze frame images of such a creeper empowering himself in somebody's house. It seemed quite clear that the editorial line was one of admiration and justification. However, a more interesting follow-up was never filmed, for it could have starred Janet Street-Porter waking up at three in the morning with a large, ethnically challenged, uninvited creeper in her home, justifying his forced entry by pointing to her media-income and stabbing her in the leg.

Ms Street-Porter would find her new-found status as a victim of crime less than satisfactory. After dialling 999, she would find the system taking over coolly and impassively, her emotions being transacted through another agency or institution. When the case reaches the courts, she may well find her position as a victim ironically up-staged by the defendant who is amply stocked with the very latest in victim-speak; complements of psychologists, social workers – and television programmes like *Network 7*. Any feelings of anger, bitterness and recrimination Ms Street-Porter might have to deal with would be processed through 'anger management', designed to help her regain a more 'healthy', 'civilised' and dispassionate perspective on the incident and the man who brought it about. It may be suggested that she 'works' out her anger via victim support self-help groups, a spot of zealous basket weaving, or if all else fails, making a TV documentary about it.

This is one of the most nauseating examples of where self-help psychology has gone terribly wrong, for the victims of crime should never be made to feel as if their enraged, extreme reactions are in the slightest way uncivilised or inappropriate, nor that they should use their intellect to override their natural inclinations. This line of thought leads to the victim becoming a victim yet again: being in some way seen as 'maladjusted' as a result of a single, isolated incident. The psychology of the criminal justice process is disease-ridden, in that those who have been attacked are left with no control over or connection with how the person responsible for their suffering is dealt with. While it may seem uncivilised to say so, this is a highly unnatural state of affairs. The unmentionable truth is that by feeling directly powerful and in control of the destiny of our attacker, being in a position to personally ensure their humiliation and to see them utterly disempowered, we are far more likely to put things in perspective and chase the ghost away. However, such a suggestion could of course *never* be entertained in our terribly civilised society.

Such political and media posturing is one facet of the mis-appropriation of a form of 'civil rights' psychology which is perceived as excusing 'alternative' forms of self-empowerment and 'social self-improvement' in the name of victimhood. It has come to the point where those who don't conceptualise racial issues the 'right' way are merely dismissed as racist. A most poignant example of this occurred recently when it was discovered by Radio 4 journalists that white, male, inner-city social workers, whilst undergoing further training, were told that before they could go any further, they had to acknowledge the fact that they were 'racist'. Those that chose not to accept this description of themselves were promptly informed that they were 'in denial'.

Even psychologists are busy accusing one another of being racist with a long-standing row still running over how racist their standard textbooks are. The guilt-ridden pages of their professional journal, *The Psychologist*, are strewn with accusations such as: 'Simply the result of their constant assault on African peoples. . . . The *net* effect of their attack on black peoples. . . . The necessity for constant vigilance on 'race' and racism. . . . Vigilance is central to anti-racism.' It appears that psychologists are feeling guilty for the wrong crime, for if they must find something to confess, it is that they are actually 'ethno-centric recidivists', viewing the world from their own white ethnic

209

background, more a case of being naive, which is quite different from being racist.

The indiscriminate use of the term 'racism' has alienated and insulted many people who are simply not 'racist' in the way that it should be understood. The moral high ground has been dominated by those who claim that we should immediately accept, without reservation, people who look very different to us. Such advisers fail to think of the reasons why people are actually *less* likely to immediately accept, without reservation, people who look very different to them. It should seem blatantly obvious to any less politically motivated observer that, in primitive times, tribal loyalties were *genetic* loyalties. ID cards, CVs and personal introductions hadn't been invented yet, and so physical appearance was the only criterion available to enable members of tribes to become immediately aware of 'outsiders' who might threaten the resources and continuity of their tribe. Such evolutionary mechanisms cannot be swept aside simply because they *appear* to be racist. The obvious fear is that by acknowledging differences, such information will be used to *discriminate* against and persecute those who are different. The same logic has been used to eradicate the use of stereotypes and generalisations: however, this attempt has also failed miserably time and time again for the same reasons. By participating in a game of mass false-consciousness, one is being asked yet again to deny and reject one's instincts and feelings. It is *not* racist to be mindful of people who are racially different, provided that one ultimately makes an informed judgement based upon that person as an individual. To demand otherwise displays an arrogant irreverence toward human nature and is simply unrealistic.

One area in which racism and exclusion are rife is that of the choice/approval of a marriage partner for our children. It was interesting to hear the views of the liberal consensus in the form of BBC Radio 4's *Any Questions?* when they addressed this issue. After the platitudes of intermarriage being wonderful and how creating 'one big racial melting pot' would ideally solve a lot of the world's problems had abated, a member of a racial minority group, in the form of Rabbi Julia Neuberger, confessed that while she was all in favour of intermarriage, on an emotional level she wanted her children to marry Jews. Her admission was met with rapturous applause because she aired what most people probably feel but would never admit in public.

Those that don't discriminate on racial grounds, discriminate on those of *class*. Arthur Scargill, former militant leader of the National Union of Mineworkers, and his wife, were reported to have some reservations about the marriage of their daughter, Margaret, to Justin Maitland, the rugby player son of John Maitland, militant president of the Australian Miners Union – one would have thought a match made in heaven. However, *Private Eye* reported that the Australian miners' boss told the Sydney press: 'Scargill and his wife aren't happy about it. It's surprising, given their background, but they seem to regard colonials with some disdain.' Mrs Maitland appeared even more forthcoming: 'When things got serious, the Scargills let it be known they disapproved; it was worse than *Guess Who's Coming to Dinner* – not just a black man, but a colonial for God's sake! And a footballer!'

The British Psychological Society does not restrict its concerns to how racist its members are. In a lead article in their journal, entitled 'Should Parents Hit Their Children?', Dr Penelope Leach argued that the profession had a responsibility to push for the outlawing of parents smacking their children: 'Physical punishment is unlikely to be effective in helping parents to shape their children's behaviour ... The use – and abuse – of parental physical punishment is unlikely to end without external intervention, such as legal change.' Dr Leach is one of the members of the Commission on Social Justice which aims to influence government policy.

We shy away from declaring people socially irredeemable. Psychological vernacular is invoked to explain and justify and goes on to hold out the promise of change. The concept of 'scum' is blasphemous and is interpreted as individuals who are 'sadly misunderstood' or 'dysfunctional'. John McVicar in an article, *Writing off the underclass*, states that the underclass, 'a parasitical and predatory cancer – are themselves the victims of high unemployment, the increasing disparities in wealth and income and, as the socialist David Downes once put it, "the Faustian experiments in social engineering of the conservative administrations since 1979". There is also something morally dubious about a suggestion that there are groups of people who are beyond reach . . . people can change.' But what of the world of underclass culture? *Untermenschen* must in future be *prevented*, for despite claims to the contrary, couched in psychological lingo, it is, in most cases, too late for a cure. One must take a close look at the world of the *Untermenschen*. This is clearly an impossibility for most white, middle-class libertarians whose only contact with such an undertribe consists of a safe encounter – with a television screen placed safely between them and the observed – or a spot of 'unpleasantness' whilst queuing in the supermarket. In a further twist of piquant irony, our libertarian friends, being so unfamiliar with day-to-day underclass culture, are rendered blissfully impervious to most of the signals which indicate the potential for 'uncivilised' behaviour. They remain happily divorced from this other world. The 'Gothic Playschool' variety of libertarians who claim they sail through Brixton or Stoke Newington without being bothered, aren't being completely honest, for if they were to dress in a more conventional, middle-class way, their time spent in Brixton or Stoke Newington would be a very different affair indeed. Women in particular are treated quite differently, being out of the frame of reference of men stabbing men, which is based upon men challenging men, men threatening men. On a street level, men are less likely to beat up or stab women and are, in fact, more deferential to them than to other men who are within their frame of reference.

There has been much talk of 'role models' and their influence on young men in particular, as Lesley White comments:

> . . . nice middle-class chaps are the last to have any impact on the lives of the alleged underclass. Middle-class children, one assumes, receive moral instruction from parents, relatives, school; but even more from an environment which rewards socially acceptable behaviour with the promise of an education and the possibility of jobs, money and security. But the would-be self-improver has no such assurances; he or she needs the example of people who have made the great journey before them. . . . Those days are gone and no number of fair footballers will bring them back. The problem is too severe. . . . The question is not so much how we can persuade young people to prefer the good guys (for we cannot) but what kind of resistance they can muster to the negative images. . . . Such children are not simply unenlightened rascals, waiting for a saintly celebrity to show them the way: they are cynical, fame-literate, locked inside their own nihilistic identity. Sure, they would change places with [Gary] Lineker tomorrow – for the money, the cars, the girls and the crack, not for the pleasure of living a more useful and fulfilled life.

This view is, however, not shared by the 'liberal intelligentsia'. A colourful example of this was to be found in an experiment carried out, not by scientists, but by well-intentioned thespians, on a rough Birmingham council estate. The local residents were offered the opportunity to express their own interpretations of

213

various Shakespearean works, all of this guided by Michael Bogdanov. Penny, the director of a TV documentary about the project, was most self-congratulatory over their ability to both prove that Shakespeare is relevant today and that they could make it accessible to these poor, unfortunate people who have no respectable Arts of their own. Incidentally, when she was introduced on Radio 4's *Start The Week* as someone who was involved in a project in a rough Birmingham inner-city council estate, she immediately put the presenter straight with the worldly observation that the crime rate for inner-city council estates is no higher than it is in Hampstead! It would have been most interesting to have introduced a little bit of competition into the project, by providing the residents with a choice between a portable theatre and a portable video arcade; or between starring in *Henry V* or drinks on the house in it; for the latter activities don't require the services of these new missionaries who desperately need the gratitude of those less fortunate than themselves.

The point of this story is that, whether such projects occur in the form of a thespian jamboree or organised video game competitions, it is actually the time, attention and concern people receive that is important – not Shakespeare. Sadly, the effects are not lasting, for when the thespians depart, they take much of the hope with them. While the short-lived social experiment made this progressive theatre company feel good about itself, the residents remain behind, and for some the reality becomes worse when they return to their normal lives: for they have seen over the precipice. Those interested in meddling in the misery of others must make it a long-term, on-going commitment, not a temporary social therapy. An example of this is provided by the Petersburn Community Library, fourteen miles from Glasgow on a bleak, graffiti-covered, Sixties council estate. For the unemployed youth who live on the estate, it has become *the* place to 'hang out'. They can borrow guitars and CDs as well as books, and there is a small video editing suite as well as a recording studio. They can make music, play computer games or learn how to write CVs: anything, as long as it is 'creative'. Reading books is not a pre-requisite. It has won a major award from the Library Association, which hailed it as the library of the future. The scheme has added weight to the idea that libraries are not just a source of free books for the chattering classes.

Another form of social therapy has reached prominence on a number of occasions. One of the most colourful examples was that of 'Mark the Safari Boy' who had been the subject of no fewer than 23 supervision orders involving more than 40 crimes committed before his eighteenth birthday. The Safari Boy was placed in the hands of Bryn Melyn Rehabilitation Centre, which helped him to undergo 'intensive individual therapeutic programmes'. One such programme involved an eighty-day 'character building' 'rehabilitation' tour of Africa. He saw the Pyramids, cruised the Nile and went on safari in Kenya. Having traversed the Dark Continent for eighty days of exotica, the Safari Boy began reoffending almost as soon as he returned home. While it is easy for newspapers to dismiss this as a foolish joke, the saddest part is that such social therapies really don't change people in the long run – because they have to ultimately return to their normal environment where nothing has changed.

It's a sign of the times that the Safari Boy's mother was keen to apportion blame for his criminal life on all the official, outside influences that tried to restrain him: his old school: 'a joke, everyone round here will tell you'; the Social Services: 'they gave him too much'; and the media: 'none of you've given him a chance' – blaming everyone for his behaviour except his *family* life. Contrary to popular belief, many young criminals actually *like* the police, who may ironically serve as male role-models;

they are perceived as caring enough to chase them and arrest them, clip them round the ear, telephone their parents; possibly in a way their parents never did and should have.

Despite the raging debate as to the causes of crime, the socio-economic excuses appropriated by the people who commit crimes and the question of how to change the behaviour of such people, there are those 'little platoons' and influential individuals who take a completely different tack – Virtual Unreality. We are encouraged *not* to believe that society is a more dangerous and hostile place nowadays and to 'reframe' our view of both the prevalence and severity of crime today. The BBC has taken part in this exercise in mass delusion, for while BBC 1 is busy transmitting *Crimewatch UK*, the libertarian documentary makers of BBC 2 are busy convincing people that things are no worse than they ever were, through the film *Forbidden Britain*, with a book by the same name. That television bible, the *Radio Times*, highlights the programme as 'Today's Choice' with an accompanying photograph (probably taken in the 1940s), of three boys wearing suits, with neatly combed hair, playing cards; the sort of 'scallywags' portrayed in the Ealing comedies; the comforting caption underneath the photo is 'So what's new? Youngsters have always found ways and means to get up to mischief.' Their social affairs columnist Polly Toynbee, who is intended to provide a 'voice of reason' perspective on current social and emotional issues, writes: 'Fear of crime, especially juvenile crime, runs deep in our veins. Violence is only five per cent of it, an exceptional phenomenon on its own . . . *Forbidden Britain* puts those alarming figures into a different perspective.' Resorting predictably to an outburst of relativism, she trots out the well-worn historical-perspective-cliché: 'We live now, and we have always lived, with the idea that each new generation coming up behind us is worse, a perpetual downward slide from some imagined golden era. . . . Each new name for the same violent youth culture spreads new alarm. Here, from the aged voices of the young offenders of yesteryear, we have a chance to see it all in a perspective that ought to frighten us less.' There is, however, some sympathy for the victims: 'The fact that someone was burgled or robbed in just the same way fifty years ago makes scant difference to their distress. But it ought to change the way we think about it and it ought to calm some of the panic this crime arouses' − *RT*.

People are certainly *not* burgled or robbed in just the same way as they were fifty years ago. Anyone who takes the time to speak to the 'chronologically disadvantaged' will hear, in no uncertain terms, that there is an enormous *qualitative* difference in the context of crime. As Britain becomes a less stratified and more mobile society, crime and criminals are able to travel out of their normal 'patches'. Moreover, people are also more wary about openly suspecting people who look and dress a certain way. They've been dissuaded from doing so as a result of the constant braying of the 'concerned' classes about the dangers of stereotypes, generalisations and, of course, racism. There is also a qualitative difference in the *nature* and the *fear* of crime. As an extreme example, the way that people in their eighties are not only robbed but are increasingly being beaten up and raped in the process. For those fortunate enough not to have to rely on buses and trains, the body language and general *atmosphere* on late night public transport, for example, is markedly different. There is a genuine air of alienation and sometimes an undertone of latent hostility.

Those who disagree that things are any more menacing nowadays may wish to explain why bus drivers are now encased in attack-resistant glass, or why bus conductors have felt the need to go on strike to draw attention to the increasing number of 'senseless' attacks on them. A 1994 Gallup survey clearly demonstrated that people feel that a concern for others and public spiritedness have declined in the last decade alone. People view those around them as being more selfish and unwilling to get involved: this even included police officers, 40 per cent of whom said they would not tell off a child if they saw it acting badly in the street. One-third of the public said that they would ignore a person lying in the street, and less than half said it was likely that they would intervene if they saw someone committing a crime. Unlike sex surveys, this survey is likely to have produced a more genuine set of responses, and if anything, has *under*estimated the state of affairs. The suggestion that we are suffering from some sort of 'False Memory Syndrome' about personal safety in previous eras and that our fears are 'all in the mind', is remarkably insulting. An extension of this line of thought is that we conspire unknowingly in creating crime, as a society we are bound up in a form of 'victimology': the fear of crime almost produces crime. As a form of social self-improvement, we are told to be more trusting. In fact, a political think-tank is working on this at the moment with a report entitled *The Politics of Trust: Reducing Fear of Crime in Urban Parks*.

While politicians, the police, the judicial system and psychologists debate crime's causes and possible solutions, it is civil engineers who appear to have provided certain interim 'solutions'. With the US crime-rate rising fast and showing no sign of abating, the ever-pragmatic Texans have implemented a new method of ensuring the security of people who come in to downtown Houston to work. A 6.3 mile private underground walkway has been dug beneath the city's pavements to provide law-abiding citizens with the opportunity to walk safely through the downtown area without the fear of crime, which in America amounts to more than mere pick-pocketing. This subterranean oasis is intended to exclude 'undesirables', i.e. obvious members of the underclass, not through any form of membership scheme or policing, but by ensuring that all entrances and exits are placed in the foyers of 'nice' institutions, such as banks and oil companies, where the *Untermenschen* would stand out like a sore thumb. It would be most interesting to know which route the likes of Polly Toynbee would take: the crime-filled streets or the non-egalitarian tunnels.

The adage 'there is no freedom without discipline' has never been more significant. It has become abundantly clear that it is imperative to at least demarcate what is the norm and to generalise from this, and even to make outright judgements. Heinous concepts such as 'rules', 'regulations', 'restrictions', 'boundaries' are strangely longed for by children and animals, moreover, if one is to rebel, one needs a structure to rebel *against*. Unfortunately, those who agree with the adage have for some time been undermined or dismissed with the ultimate 'insult' of being 'right wing', a political philistine, rather partial to Back-To-Basics philosophies. A marvellous way to eliminate those whose ideas differ. Such people have managed to appropriate the term 'liberal' for their own brand of conformist thinking. As Stephen Amidon asks, 'How is it that liberalism, the noblest credo to flower from the rational imagination of man, has become the scapegoat of political and cultural discourse? Why has this once vital philosophy become a moribund ideology? . . . Whereas conservatism finds its essence in unwavering truisms . . . liberalism holds that human intellect, working in concert with other free minds, can solve problems as they occur.' Like science, liberalism was intended as a way of thinking, not a specific ideology. It explored ways in which the individual could engage reason to maintain his liberty. Amidon remarks:'This flexibility was always liberalism's strong suit, allowing it to slay the dragon of dogmatism time and time again.' The political right has always been openly intransigent and authoritarian, and it is, in some ways, less dangerous and pernicious. Many of those who have marched under the banner of 'liberalism' have, on the other hand, displayed the most convoluted interpretation of liberal thinking, understanding and tolerance, protected by a most effective political camouflage. A redefinition of the term 'liberal' is long overdue, for it should be reclaimed by those willing to consider *all* perspectives, be they pleasant, fashionable or not.

The current trend finds that, like the former Nazis who disclaimed any responsibility for ushering in Nazism, members of the liberal intelligentsia are now engaged in a public dismissal and attack upon political correctness. The most active area of debate is between the two biggest consumers of misappropriated psychology: liberals and the left. Right-wing polemics against PC are obvious and predictable. There are those who were quite happy to usher in and validate PC thinking when it was considered a form of radical chic; aligning themselves with what were perceived as alternative formalised anti-Establishment and liberating trends. However, once it became fashionable and slightly provocative to turn against PC, they hopped straight on that bandwagon as well; with Sarah Dunant, for instance, now publishing a book on *The Political Correctness Debate* . . . published by Virago – of course.

11: The Way it Is

A sense of sobriety is long overdue: the reinstatement of a realistic sense of balance between notions of 'personal responsibility' and other influences in determining one's thoughts, feelings and behaviours.

There are parallels and overlaps between the worlds of public psychology and the more recent trend in encouraging people to take more responsibility for their own health and medical conditions (the 'well-being movement'). The Israeli health scientist Professor Aaron Antonovsky of Ben-Gurion University has recently expressed serious reservations about the well-being movement. He now believes that it has conveniently paid undue attention to matters of personal responsibility and the self when it comes to health and illness without adequately acknowledging the corporate and social context. He feels this is either a remarkably naive stance to adopt or else a rather sinister trend which shifts responsibility for health from those involved in policy-making to the individual. In short, it is thought that there is too much 'self' in the well-being movement and the studies that surround it, and not enough social responsibility.

This is not to say that a little more individual responsibility is at all a bad thing for the British who have, for too long, been lulled into believing that the 'experts' will tell them what needs to be done about their health and, more recently, their emotional well-being. In fact, good old-fashioned health education has been working (somewhat unsuccessfully) toward this end for some time now. While notions of 'taking responsibility' and 'individualism' have a rather democratic and fashionable ring about them, they can also be used to disempower the individual. By providing the apparent means of achieving and maintaining health and well-being through, for example, corporate programmes, it is possible to put the employee's state of health down to the individual and to apportion any blame accordingly.

Psychology cannot 'empower' us to overcome our limitations, be they genetic, developmental or age-related, therefore accepting our limitations is not, as many would have us believe, a defeatist attitude to adopt. Contrary to many of the ideas that have been extracted from psychology, it is actually far more likely to provide any genuine sense of 'self-fulfilment', 'empowerment' etc. For most people, the best you can hope for is being able to know yourself better. This may seem a modest aspiration given the enticing possibilities presented over the past thirty years, yet it remains the most tried and tested way of experiencing the least amount of bewilderment and pain. While self-acceptance – making the best of a bad job – would appear the ideal state of affairs, even this is in effect a form of change, which does not come easy. Popeye's ability to state most confidently, 'I am what I am what I am what I am' is a gift.

The emphasis on resorting to externally derived approaches to living has produced little and dramatically increased the gap between our expectations and reality. Before consulting celebrated authorities, we would be better advised to turn to the best source of free advice regarding navel gazing – your friendly neighbourhood old age pensioners. Introspection takes *time*: something recent generations do not seem to have time for. Yet, like trying to bake a birthday cake in a microwave oven, there is no way to condense the process: you cannot hot-house emotional development. The much discouraged practice of daydreaming, letting thoughts and feelings wander unfettered, at one time provided people with at least an opportunity to 'get in touch with their emotions' in a natural, more uncontrived way. Nowadays, such a 'waste of otherwise constructive time' can be better spent in a very unnatural and contrived way through, for example, watching television.

However, there have recently been attempts to change the public face of day-dreaming and general idleness: a movement dedicated to the lost art of taking it easy. There has even been a magazine, *The Idler*, described by its editor, Tom Hodgkinson, as intended 'to express this new culture'. Hodgkinson notes that 'Advertising hoardings bellow "Go For It" or "Just Do It". In conversation the innocuous "How are you?" is often followed with "Keeping busy?" or "Working hard?" as if business is next to happiness. . . . We want to turn the dominant guiding ideas – work is good, sloth is bad – upside down, and encourage a culture where the opposite is true, where manic working is seen for what it often is: a sign of some unresolved inner conflict, a lack of creativity, of spirituality, of self-knowledge. We want a culture where you don't have to pretend to the boss that you are working when you are not; where you don't have to take guilty naps at your desk. In an idler's world, the emphasis will be on quality of work rather than speed of execution and hours put in.' Given the nature of this movement, it may be quite some time before people can be bothered to take to the streets to declare their lack of enthusiasm for things.

Previously, society was more spacious, both geographically and emotionally. One was able to *lose* oneself. Now, however, with the telephone and television in every house, we are enveloped by a sense of omnipresence: man-made claustrophobia. Moreover, the enthusiasm for an ever more global village may, in retrospect, be seen as misguided, for while the public may enjoy the fruits of such expansion in the form of baseball caps, karaoke, Kentucky Fried Chicken and Bud, it is questionable whether humans are able to comprehend and cope with such a global, large-scale view of society – a false sense of a 'world community'. In his book *Amusing Ourselves to Death*, the academic Neil Postman warned of the effects that television would have in creating such a global village. The idea of decontextualised information being transmitted around the world in nano-seconds depicting events, values and lifestyles which one has little connection with and even less control over, only adds to an ever-growing sense of impotence and inadequacy – the Tiannamen Square massacre, brought to you by CNN.

What is consistently overlooked is that our minds and, for that matter, our bodies are best suited to a world long gone, a world which was relatively consistent, stable and unchanging, whose dangers were clearly definable, recognisable and immediate, as opposed to ambiguous and chronic. Social, economic and technological change, even for the good, has profound biological and psychological consequences for the individual and society and is at the heart of the pressures of modern life. Such change, if anything, is likely to accelerate in the future. To what extent do we, as individuals, *really* have any control over events, and choice over the way we respond emotionally to such events?

Like the need to take time, people need to take space to lose themselves, and not just for two weeks every summer. Predictably, psychology has a nomenclature for losing oneself by spending more time outdoors: 'eco-psychology'. But unfortunately, unless one is in the business of selling either pocket watches or package holidays, attempting to sell time and space is not a particularly lucrative endeavour.

Despite the fashionable reservations about therapy and counselling, such approaches do have their places and the beneficial effects should not be discounted. Given the fact that we do live in a more alienated society where not only has the extended family become virtually extinct, and even the nuclear family is rapidly becoming a minority group; counselling and therapy fulfil a very important function in filling the void left by fewer shoulders to cry on. While these professions are described by some as being comprised of 'paid listeners', there is a terrible need for *someone* to listen to you when you are suffering emotional distress. Furthermore, we can possibly gain a more objective perspective from someone outside one's own frame of reference. Whether the particular therapy is in itself responsible for helping someone in need, is another question altogether.

But before one resorts to sending an SAE to EXIT, it's important to realise that there is consolation to be found in pain, misery, loneliness and other dysfunctional states. Moreover, society is dependent upon such maladjustments for its entertainment. A number of long-term studies have concluded that the image of the tortured genius suffering for his art, having lost his mind in a fog of 'clinical mood disorders', sexual problems and alcoholism, actually appears to be *true*. One study by Dr Felix Post, formerly of the Maudsley Hospital, was published in the *British Journal of Psychiatry* and examined the lives of nearly 300 famous men considered exceptionally creative, and concluded that psychiatric abnormalities do play a role in generating creativity of the highest order. Other studies have supported these findings. Severe personality disorders were found to occur considerably more often in novelists or dramatists, composers and artists than in scientists, politicians and intellectuals. Although the study did not include women and was restricted to the past 150 years, it was mentioned that Charlotte Brontë, George Eliot, Virginia Woolf and Marie Curie all had serious psychiatric or psycho-sexual problems. It also revealed that 31 per cent of composers, 37 per cent of painters and 46 per cent of writers suffered from severe psychopathologies. Composers included Wagner, Tchaikovsky, Schumann, Rachmaninov, Puccini, Elgar and Berlioz. Painters included Cézanne, Munch, Picasso, Rossetti, Turner and Van Gogh. Writers included Conrad, Faulkner, Gide, Hemingway, Joyce, Kipling, Proust, Scott Fitzgerald, Tolstoy, Waugh and

Wells. Dr Post stated: 'As the most surprising finding of the investigation, 72 per cent of novelists and playwrights suffered from depressive conditions.'

Creativity is not, however, the only desirable quality associated with social and emotional perils. As a cartoon by Rona Chadwick reads: 'I am active, adventurous, aggressive, assertive, curious, energetic, enterprising, frank, independent and inventive. Needless to say, this hasn't won me many friends.'

Selected Bibliography

Abels, Kathleen, cited in *The Mating Game* by William F. Allman, US News & World

Amidon, Stephen, 'The Closing of the Liberal Mind' *Sunday Times*, 6.11.94

Appleyard, Brian, 'Created in Man's Own Image' *Independent*, 6.7.94

Argyle, Michael, *The Psychology of Social Class*, Routledge, 1994

Beauman, Sally, 'Labours of Love', *Sunday Times*, 6.11.94

Briscoe, Joanna 'Lipstick on her Collar', *Sunday Times*, 5.6.94

Carruthers, Malcolm, cited in 'The Male Hormone Behind All Successful Women' by Chrissie Iley, *Sunday Times*, 4.9.94

Chadwick, Rona, Active And Adventurous Cath Tate Cards 1988

Chopra, Deepak, *Ageless Body, Timeless Mind – The Quantum Alternative to Growing Old*, Harmony Books 1993

Cooper, Cary, cited in 'I know A Man Who Does' by Katharine Hadley, *Sunday Times*, 6.11.94

Crosland, Susan, 'Whatever Happened To Those Devoted Sisters?', *Evening Standard*, 13.7.94

D'Souza, Christa, 'Sleeping Partners', *Sunday Times*, 28.8.94

Davies, John B, 'Seeds of a False Consciousness', *The Psychologist*, August 1994

Dejevsky, Mary, 'Why *Windows* is a Feminist Issue', *Independent* 2.9.94

Disney, 'Leadership Disney Style – Managers Guide' Euro Disney University 1993

Fairley, Josephine, 'The Truth About Female Ejaculation', *Cosmopolitan*, December 1993

Farrington, David, cited in 'Media Watch', *The Psychologist*, August 1994

Fenwick, E; Walker, R, *Family Planning Association – How Sex Works*, Dorling Kindersley, 1994

Fisher, Nick, *Health Education Authority – Your Pocket Guide to Sex*, Health Education Authority, 1994

Goldenson, R; Anderson, K, *The Wordsworth Dictionary of Sex*, Wordsworth Editions Ltd, 1994

Hadley, Katharine, 'I Know A Man Who Does', *Sunday Times*, 6.11.94

Hamblin, Ken, cited in 'Ken Hamblin, black scourge', *The Economist*, 5.2.94

Hickson, Ford. 'Symposium on Psychological Issues in Gay Male Sexuality' Annual Conference of the British Psychological Society, April, 1993 reported by Adrian Coyle in *The Psychologist*, July 1993

Hilgard, E R, Atkinson, R C & Atkinson R L, *Introduction to Psychology*, Harcourt Brace Jovanovich, 1975

Hodgkinson, Tom, 'Positively Idle' *Guardian* 9.11.94

Jackson, Patterson & Young 'Fuck The Police' by Niggaz With Attitude, Ruthless Attack Muzick (USA)

Kane, Pat, 'Putting Us All in the Picture' *Sunday Times*, 28.8.94

Knight, Lindsay, 'Assert Yourself', Channel 4 Television, 1987

Leach, Penelope, 'Should Parents Hit Their Children?' *The Psychologist*, May 1993

Littig, Lawrence, 'Rating Tattoos', *The Psychologist*, October 1994

Litvinoff, Sarah, *The Relate Guide to Better Relationships*, Vermilion, 1994

Litvinoff, Sarah, *The Relate Guide to Sex in Loving Relationships*, Vermilion, 1993

Litvinoff, Sarah, *The Relate Guide to Starting Again*, Vermilion, 1993

Mackintosh, N J, 'The Biology of Intelligence?' *British Journal of*

Psychology 77, 1–18, 1986

McVicar, John, 'Writing Off the Underclass in Weasel Words', *Sunday Times*, 4.9.94

Mason, Michael, *The Making of Victorian Sexual Attitudes*, Oxford University Press, 1994

Masson, Jeffrey, *Against Therapy*, Harper Collins, 1992

Mitchell, Margaret, 'Media Watch', *The Psychologist*, October 1994

Mitchell, Warren, cited in 'Nasty Work If You Can Get It' by James Rampton, *Independent*, 25.10.94

Osborne, John, 'Cream Teas, Bile and the Lower Middle Classes' *Mail on Sunday*, 14.8.94

Patten, John, quoted in 'Boys Get Their Own Classes to Catch Up' by Charles Hymas, *Sunday Times*, 10.7.94

Peters, T; Austin, N K, *A Passion for Excellence: The Leadership Difference*, Random House, 1984

Peters, Tom; Waterman, B, *In the Search of Excellence*, Harper & Row, 1982

Peters, Tom, *The Excellence Challenge* (Audio Cassette), Nightingale–Conant Corporation, 1984

Plomin, Robert, cited in 'Gene Rebels with a Cause' by Jerome Burne, *Independent*, 20.10.94

Porter, Roy, 'Child's Play', *Sunday Times*, 4.9.94

Price, John, 'Self–Esteem' *The Lancet*, 1988, Oct Issue: 8617 pp 943–944

Puplampu, Bill, 'The Psychology of Development', *The Psychologist*, November 1994

Rabbitt, Patrick, cited in 'Let's Face The Music And Rot' by Brian Appleyard, *Independent*, 7.9.94

Radford, John, 'Psychology and its Students', *The Psychologist*, October 1994

Reichel, Sabine, 'Some Women Seem To Relish Misery in Marriage', *Los Angeles Times*, 20.1.94

Roberts, Yvonne, *Every Woman Deserves an Adventure*, Macmillan, 1994

Rogers, Buck, *Excellence in Action* (Audio Cassette), Nightingale–Conant Corporation, 1984

Senge, Peter, cited in 'The Real Meaning of Empowerment' by Jane Pickard, *Personnel Management*, November 1993

Silver, Rachel, *Where Their Feet Dance: English Women's Sexual Fantasies*, Century, 1994

Smith, Joan, *Misogynies*, Faber & Faber, 1989

Speight, Johnny, cited in 'Nasty Work If You Can Get It' by James Rampton, *Independent*, 25.10.94

Symons, D., *The Evolution of Human Sexuality*, Oxford University Press, 1979

Thomas, David, 'A Year of Living Dangerously', *Sunday Times*, 21.11.93

Tylczak, L, *Downsizing Without Disaster*, Crisp Publications Inc, 1991

White, Lesley, 'Even The Golden Boy Is No Match for Yob Culture', *Sunday Times*, 25.9.94

Zohar, Danah, 'How Science Shows Religion The Way', *Sunday Times*, 14.8.94